THE CHRYSOSTOM BIBLE
A Commentary Series for Preaching and Teaching
Joshua: A Commentary

THE CHRYSOSTOM BIBLE
A Commentary Series for Preaching and Teaching

Joshua: A Commentary

Paul Nadim Tarazi

OCABS PRESS
ST PAUL, MINNESOTA 55124
2013

THE CHRYSOSTOM BIBLE
JOSHUA: A COMMENTARY

ISBN 1-60191-019-3

PRINTED IN THE UNITED STATES OF AMERICA

For

Archbishop Philip Saliba
of North America

and

Archbishop George Khodr
of Mount Lebanon

Other Books by the Author

I Thessalonians: A Commentary

Galatians: A Commentary

The Old Testament: An Introduction

Volume 1: Historical Traditions, revised edition

Volume 2: Prophetic Traditions

Volume 3: Psalms and Wisdom

The New Testament: An Introduction

Volume 1: Paul and Mark

Volume 2: Luke and Acts

Volume 3: Johannine Writings

Volume 4: Matthew and the Canon

The Chrysostom Bible

Genesis: A Commentary

Philippians: A Commentary

Romans: A Commentary

Colossians & Philemon: A Commentary

1 Corinthians: A Commentary

Ezekiel: A Commentary

Land and Covenant

The Chrysostom Bible
Joshua: A Commentary

ISBN 1-60191-019-3

Published by OCABS Press, St. Paul, Minnesota.
Printed in the United States of America.

Books are available through OCABS Press at special discounts
for bulk purchases in the United States by academic institutions,
churches, and other organizations. For more information please
email OCABS Press at press@ocabs.org.

Abbreviations

Books by the Author

1 Thess   *1 Thessalonians: A Commentary,* Crestwood, NY: St. Vladimir's Seminary Press, 1982

Gal   *Galatians: A Commentary,* Crestwood, NY: St. Vladimir's Seminary Press, 1994

OTI₁   *The Old Testament: An Introduction, Volume 1: Historical Traditions,* revised edition, Crestwood, NY: St. Vladimir's Seminary Press, 2003

OTI₂   *The Old Testament: An Introduction, Volume 2: Prophetic Traditions,* Crestwood, NY: St. Vladimir's Seminary Press, 1994

OTI₃   *The Old Testament: An Introduction, Volume 3: Psalms and Wisdom,* Crestwood, NY: St. Vladimir's Seminary Press, 1996

NTI₁   *The New Testament: An Introduction, Volume 1: Paul and Mark,* Crestwood, NY: St. Vladimir's Seminary Press, 1999

NTI₂   *The New Testament: An Introduction, Volume 2: Luke and Acts,* Crestwood, NY: St. Vladimir's Seminary Press, 2001

NTI₃   *The New Testament: An Introduction, Volume 3: Johannine Writings,* Crestwood, NY: St. Vladimir's Seminary Press, 2004

NTI₄   *The New Testament: An Introduction, Volume 4: Matthew and the Canon,* St. Paul, MN: OCABS Press, 2009

C-Gen   *Genesis: A Commentary.* The Chrysostom Bible. St. Paul, MN: OCABS Press, 2009

C-Phil   *Philippians: A Commentary.* The Chrysostom Bible. St. Paul, MN: OCABS Press, 2009

C-Rom   *Romans: A Commentary.* The Chrysostom Bible. St. Paul, MN: OCABS Press, 2010

C-Col   *Colossians & Philemon: A Commentary.* The Chrysostom Bible. St. Paul, MN: OCABS Press, 2010

C-1Cor   *1 Corinthians: A Commentary.* The Chrysostom Bible. St. Paul, MN: OCABS Press, 2011

C-Ezek   *Ezekiel: A Commentary.* The Chrysostom Bible. St. Paul, MN: OCABS Press, 2012

LAC   *Land and Covenant,* St. Paul, MN: OCABS Press, 2009

Abbreviations

*Books of the Old Testament**

Gen	Genesis	Job	Job	Hab	Habakkuk
Ex	Exodus	Ps	Psalms	Zeph	Zephaniah
Lev	Leviticus	Prov	Proverbs	Hag	Haggai
Num	Numbers	Eccl	Ecclesiastes	Zech	Zechariah
Deut	Deuteronomy	Song	Song of Solomon	Mal	Malachi
Josh	Joshua	Is	Isaiah	Tob	Tobit
Judg	Judges	Jer	Jeremiah	Jdt	Judith
Ruth	Ruth	Lam	Lamentations	Wis	Wisdom
1 Sam	1 Samuel	Ezek	Ezekiel	Sir Sirach	(Ecclesiasticus)
2 Sam	2 Samuel	Dan	Daniel	Bar	Baruch
1 Kg	1 Kings	Hos	Hosea	1 Esd	1 Esdras
2 Kg	2 Kings	Joel	Joel	2 Esd	2 Esdras
1 Chr	1 Chronicles	Am	Amos	1 Macc	1 Maccabees
2 Chr	2 Chronicles	Ob	Obadiah	2 Macc	2 Maccabees
Ezra	Ezra	Jon	Jonah	3 Macc	3 Maccabees
Neh	Nehemiah	Mic	Micah	4 Macc	4 Maccabees
Esth	Esther	Nah	Nahum		

Books of the New Testament

Mt	Matthew	Eph	Ephesians	Heb	Hebrews
Mk	Mark	Phil	Philippians	Jas	James
Lk	Luke	Col	Colossians	1 Pet	1 Peter
Jn	John	1 Thess	1 Thessalonians	2 Pet	2 Peter
Acts	Acts	2 Thess	2 Thessalonians	1 Jn	1 John
Rom	Romans	1 Tim	1 Timothy	2 Jn	2 John
1 Cor	1 Corinthians	2 Tim	2 Timothy	3 Jn	3 John
2 Cor	2 Corinthians	Titus	Titus	Jude	Jude
Gal	Galatians	Philem	Philemon	Rev	Revelation

Following the larger canon known as the Septuagint.

Contents

Preface

The present Bible Commentary Series is not so much in honor of John Chrysostom as it is to continue and promote his legacy as an interpreter of the biblical texts for preaching and teaching God's congregation, in order to prod its members to proceed on the way they started when they accepted God's calling. Chrysostom's virtual uniqueness is that he did not subscribe to any hermeneutic or methodology, since this would amount to introducing an extra-textual authority over the biblical texts. For him, scripture is its own interpreter. Listening to the texts time and again allowed him to realize that "call" and "read (aloud)" are not interconnected realities; rather, they are one reality since they both are renditions of the same Hebrew verb *qara'*. Given that words read aloud are words of instruction for one "to do them," the only valid reaction would be to hear, listen, obey, and abide by these words. All these connotations are subsumed in the same Hebrew verb *šama'*. On the other hand, these scriptural "words of life" are presented as readily understandable utterances of a father to his children (Isaiah 1:2-3). The recipients are never asked to engage in an intellectual debate with their divine instructor, or even among themselves, to fathom what he is saying. The Apostle to the Gentiles followed in the footsteps of the Prophets to Israel by handing down to them the Gospel, that is, the Law of God's Spirit through his Christ (Romans 8:2; Galatians 6:2) as fatherly instruction (1 Corinthians 4:15). He in turn wrote readily understandable letters to be read aloud. It is in these same footsteps that Chrysostom followed, having learned from both the Prophets and Paul that the same "words of life" carry also the sentence of death at the hand of the scriptural God, Judge of all

(Deuteronomy 28; Joshua 8:32-35; Psalm 82; Matthew 3:4-12; Romans 2:12-16; 1 Corinthians 10:1-11; Revelation 20:11-15).

While theological debates and hermeneutical theories come and go after having fed their proponents and their fans with passing human glory, the Golden Mouth's expository homilies, through the centuries, fed and still feed myriads of believers in so many traditions and countries. Virtually banned from dogmatic treatises, he survives in the hearts of "those who have ears to hear." His success is due to his commitment to exegesis rather than to futile hermeneutics. The latter behaves as someone who dictates on a living organism what it is supposed to be, whereas exegesis submits to that organism and endeavors to decipher it through trial and error. There is as much a far cry between the text and the theories about it as there is between a living organism and the theories about it. The biblical texts are the reality of God imparted through their being read aloud in the midst of the congregation, disregarding the value of the sermon that follows. The sermon, much less a theological treatise, is at best an invitation to hear and obey the text. Assessing the shape of an invitation card has no value whatsoever when it comes to the dinner itself; the guests are fed by the dinner, not by the invitation or its phrasing (Luke 14:16-24; Matthew 22:1-14).

This commentary series does not intend to promote Chrysostom's ideas as a public relation manager would do, but rather to follow in the footsteps of his approach as true children and heirs are expected to do. He used all the contemporary tools at his disposal to communicate God's written instruction to his hearers, as a doctor would with his patients, without spending unnecessary energy on peripheral debates requiring the use of professional jargon incomprehensible to the commoner. The writers of this series will try to do the same: muster to the best of their ability all necessary contemporary knowledge to communicate to the general readers the biblical message without burdening them with data unnecessary for that purpose. Whenever it will be deemed necessary or even helpful to do so, and in order to curtail burdensome and lengthy technical asides within the commentaries, specialized monographs related either to specific topics or to the scriptural background—literary, socio-political, or archeological—will be issued as companions to the series.

Paul Nadim Tarazi
Editor

Introduction

The Book of Joshua within Scripture

As is the case with most of scripture, the study of the Book of Joshua has been plagued by the proof texting approach of classical theology in all its shades. Instead of asking the simple question, "What is the book saying?" most of us have been programmed to ask, "What is the book saying concerning a certain topic?" The trouble with the latter question is not so much the issue of its theoretical validity, but rather that the "topic" we are interested in is already defined in our minds; the result is that, by merely asking the question, we are already straightjacketing scripture. Instead of allowing scripture to define its own vocabulary in order for us to understand *its* point of view, our question imposes an answer even if scripture is not dealing at all with the "topic" we are concerned with. In two previous commentaries, I have shown how detrimental such a faulty approach is. In the case of Ezekiel, because RSV, which was produced after World War II, assumed the correctness of political Zionism, it understood that book as dealing with the "land" of Israel as a piece of an actual real estate, and consequently leveled the difference between *'adamah* (ground) and *'ereṣ* (earth) rendering both into "land" and even supplementing an additional "own" that is not extant in the original:

> Thus says the Lord God: When I gather the house of Israel from the peoples among whom they are scattered, and manifest my holiness in them in the sight of the nations, then they shall dwell in *their own land* (*'admatam*; their ground) which I gave to my servant Jacob. (28:25)

21

Son of man, when the house of Israel dwelt in *their own land* (*'admatam*; their ground), they defiled it by their ways and their doings; their conduct before me was like the uncleanness of a woman in her impurity. (36:17)

For I will take you from the nations, and gather you from all the countries, and bring you into *your own land* (*'admatkem*; your ground). (36:24)

And I will put my Spirit within you, and you shall live, and I will place you in *your own land* (*'admatkem*; your ground); then you shall know that I, the Lord, have spoken, and I have done it, says the Lord. (37:14)

Then say to them, Thus says the Lord God: Behold, I will take the people of Israel from the nations among which they have gone, and will gather them from all sides, and bring them to *their own land* (*'admatam*; their ground). (37:21)

Then they shall know that I am the Lord their God because I sent them into exile among the nations, and then gathered them into *their own land* (*'admatam*; their ground). I will leave none of them remaining among the nations any more. (39:28)

Similarly, in my discussion of 2 Corinthians 4 I have shown that the original meaning of divine "glory" was misconstrued under the influence of the later Patristic understanding of that noun.

Still, in order to understand what a given biblical book is saying one needs to hear that book *within the totality of scripture*, that is to say, as that book stands within the scriptural canon. The reason is that it is linked to what comes both before it and after it. Let me give two striking examples from Joshua itself. At the end of the book, right after the mention of the death and burial of Joshua (24:30-31) we unexpectedly hear: "The bones of Joseph which the people of Israel brought up from Egypt were buried at Shechem, in the portion of ground which Jacob bought from the sons of Hamor the father of Shechem for a hundred pieces of money; it became an inheritance of the descendants of Joseph." (v.32) This passage clearly harks back 147 chapters to an earlier scriptural story: "And Moses took the bones of Joseph with him; for Joseph had solemnly sworn the people of Israel, saying, 'God will visit you; then you must carry my bones with you from here.'"(Ex 13:19) On the other hand, the story concerning the covenant with the Gibeonites and its lasting value (Josh 9) does not find its denouement until the end of 2 Samuel:

Now there was a famine in the days of David for three years, year after year; and David sought the face of the Lord. And the Lord said, "There is bloodguilt on Saul and on his house, because he put the Gibeonites to death." So the king called the Gibeonites. Now the Gibeonites were not of the people of Israel, but of the remnant of the Amorites; although the people of Israel had sworn to spare them, Saul had sought to slay them in his zeal for the people of Israel and Judah. And David said to the Gibeonites, "What shall I do for you? And how shall I make expiation, that you may bless the heritage of the Lord?" The Gibeonites said to him, "It is not a matter of silver or gold between us and Saul or his house; neither is it for us to put any man to death in Israel." And he said, "What do you say that I shall do for you?" They said to the king, "The man who consumed us and planned to destroy us, so that we should have no place in all the territory of Israel, let seven of his sons be given to us, so that we may hang them up before the Lord at Gibeon on the mountain of the Lord." And the king said, "I will give them." But the king spared Mephibosheth, the son of Saul's son Jonathan, because of the oath of the Lord which was between them, between David and Jonathan the son of Saul. The king took the two sons of Rizpah the daughter of Aiah, whom she bore to Saul, Armoni and Mephibosheth; and the five

sons of Merab the daughter of Saul, whom she bore to Adriel the
son of Barzillai the Meholathite; and he gave them into the hands
of the Gibeonites, and they hanged them on the mountain before
the Lord, and the seven of them perished together. They were put
to death in the first days of harvest, at the beginning of barley
harvest. (21:1-9)

If one applies the same approach to the so-called "conquest or
possession of the promised land" in Joshua, this title will prove
to be a misnomer. It is precisely because the scriptural Israel
mistook God's gift of "inheritance" as communal "possession" or
"property," that the Lord will dispossess the "children of Israel"
of his gift to them at the end of 2 Kings. Beyond that, the hearer
will have to wait patiently until the end of Ezekiel to understand
what the "ground of Israel" was supposed to be: a pasture land
open to all around the one city "the Lord is there" (Ezek 48).
And lest the hearers miss the moral of the scriptural story, the
following book, the scroll of the Twelve Prophets, ends on the
following note:

> Remember the law of my servant Moses, the statutes and
> ordinances that I commanded him at Horeb for all Israel. Behold,
> I will send you Elijah the prophet before the great and terrible day
> of the Lord comes. And he will turn the hearts of fathers to their
> children and the hearts of children to their fathers, lest I come and
> smite the land (ha'areṣ; the earth) with a curse. (Mal 4:4-6)

Thus, not only the Prior Prophets (Joshua, Judges, Samuel and
Kings) are to be heard as a unit, but the entire prophetic section
of scripture—the Latter Prophets (Isaiah, Jeremiah, Ezekiel, the
Twelve) as well as the Prior Prophets—is to be taken as
overarching literature. Still, since not only the beginning of
Joshua, but also the end of Malachi, refer to the Law of Moses,
then the entirety of the Law and the Prophets (Mt 5:17; 7:12;

22:40) are to be taken together, the first introducing the second and the second consistently harking back to the first. The corollary is that Joshua and Deuteronomy, i.e., the first book in the Prophets and the last book in the Law, function together as a hinge between the two scriptural units. When Joshua is heard within the entire canonical range of the Law and the Prophets, it becomes clear that the false premise of "conquest and possession of the land," let alone the understanding of land as a deeded property, will prove untenable.

Could one find a reason behind so blatant a mishearing of scripture? In the Introduction to my *Philippians: A Commentary* I have argued that an equally false premise in classical theology led to a total mishandling of scripture. Since the root *theolog*—in both its nominal and verbal forms is not extant either in the LXX or the New Testament, so-called "theology" was bound to straightjacket scripture. Whereas scripture deals with God's "plan" (*oikonomia*) of salvation, the theological endeavor relegated such to a secondary interest, and chose the mainly Platonic and Plotinic philosophical approach to delve into pontifications concerning the "deity," which inescapably led to unwarranted divisions within God's *one* church. Theology did what scripture explicitly forbade in 1 Corinthians. Oblivious to Paul's unequivocal understanding of the phrase "knowledge of God" as shorthand for "knowledge of his *will*" (Col 1:9-10) inscribed in the Law, theologians indulged in gratuitous mental debates as to *our* correct understanding of what *God is all about* even in his so-called eternal existence before creation, that is, before the implementation of his "plan" with which scripture is concerned. Whereas the Law purposely starts at Genesis 1:1, theology overbids scripture by investigating a fictional realm that supposedly *precedes* the "beginning" of the scriptural story and thus "created" another "beginning" before it.[1] Put otherwise, theology followed the path delineated in the original Greek *theologia*, discourse (*logos*) about or concerning God, when, in fact, scripture contained the discourse of God (*logos tou Theou*) addressed to the hearers as statutes and commandments to *walk by* in order to *live by* them.[2] Theologians followed in the footsteps of philosophers who presented their own discourse, philosophy, as *the truth* that guides us to how to *walk* our life. Similarly theologians made of their own discourse, theology, *the way* to salvation and life eternal, contravening the express teaching of Jesus Christ in Matthew: "But you are not to be called rabbi, for you have one teacher, and you are all brethren. And call no man your father on earth, for you have one Father, who is in heaven. *Neither be called masters, for you have one master, the Christ.*" (23:8-10) And in order to forego any misinterpretation of these words and, by the same token, preempt any further *discourse over* them, the same Jesus Christ authoritatively concludes his teaching in this Gospel thus: "Go therefore and make disciples of all nations ... teaching them to *observe* all that *I have commanded* you; and lo, I am with you always, to the close of the age." (20:19a, 20) Christ's teaching is a Torah, commandments to be observed in our daily lives as is evident already in chapters 5-7, and not "thoughts" to be discussed by and among ourselves.[3] Yet, unfortunately, instead of

---

[1] Pun intended.

[2] See, e.g., Ezek 11:17-21; 36:24-27; 37:24.

[3] In Mt 16: 23 Jesus scolds Peter, who was giving his "opinion" to him, with these words: "Get behind me, Satan! You are a hindrance to me; for you do not think the matters of God (according to God), but those of men (according to men" (my translation). JB has: "Get behind me, Satan! You are an obstacle in my path, because you are thinking not as God thinks but as human beings do." RSV has "Get behind me, Satan! You are a hindrance to me; for you are not on the side of God, but of men." KJV has "Get thee behind me, Satan: thou art an offence unto me: for thou savourest not the things that be of God, but those that be of men." RSV has the

the nations, equated more specifically with the Hellenes (Greeks) in scripture, submitting to scripture, theologians opted to treat the scripture as though it were of the same fabric as Plato's dialogues, that is, consisting of propositions to be debated.

When confronted with the scriptural stories of wars, conquests, and victories, the same Greco-Roman minds followed a similar course; instead of hearing them as an integral part of the entire *one* scriptural odyssey, the "theologians" gave them a value on their own ground as though those stories were propositions to be debated and, eventually, to which "satisfying" solutions were to be found. Still, given the "crassness" of those stories, which were reminiscent of the Iliad, the Christian intellectual tradition followed the way of Plato who "demythologized" the Iliad's stories in order to save them as part of the patrimony of the same Hellenes he was trying to educate. Such a demythologizing effort in theology sounded all the more necessary given the extreme position of the second century Marcion who opted for outright dismissal of the Old Testament. In order to salvage the Book of Joshua—the Old Testament "Jesus"—the Christian intellectual tradition "spiritualized" it into a story prefiguring the Jesus of the New Testament, a story of cleansing of sins. However, by so doing, the Book of Joshua was given an "ultimate" value per se and thus was robbed of its functional position within the total scriptural story.[4]

Still, the irony is that, whenever it suited them, the same Greco-Romans read "factually" the stories contained in Joshua and de facto ended up opting for Achilles' panoply over that of

---

loosest rendering: "Get behind me, Satan! You are a hindrance to me; for you are not on the side of God, but of men."

[4] Such is not a singular instance. The same fate befell the Book of Job that was read christologically and thus misread.

God and for Achilles' shield over the shield of trust (faith) in God's teaching inscribed in scripture and preached by Paul among the Gentiles in terms of "the gospel of peace":

> Finally, be strong in the Lord and in the strength of his might. Put on the whole armor of God, that you may be able to stand against the wiles of the devil. For we are not contending against flesh and blood, but against the principalities, against the powers, against the world rulers of this present darkness, against the spiritual hosts of wickedness in the heavenly places. Therefore take the whole armor of God, that you may be able to withstand in the evil day, and having done all, to stand. Stand therefore, having girded your loins with truth, and having put on the breastplate of righteousness, and having shod your feet with the equipment of the gospel of peace; besides all these, taking the shield of faith, with which you can quench all the flaming darts of the evil one. And take the helmet of salvation, and the sword of the Spirit, which is the word of God. (Eph 6:10-17)

In other words, they overlooked that the *sword* of the Spirit was nothing other than the *word* of God which, as a "light to the nations," invites the enemies to submit to God's will without coercing them (Is 2:2-4). In this sense the misreading of the scriptural stories of war and conquest produced more detrimental results than the misreading of the so-called "christological" and "theological" passages. The latter, to be sure, was behind internecine battles among Christians, always with the acknowledgment that such battles "ought not to have happened." However, the former misreading bloodied Christian history with literal, and often unwarranted, aggressive extermination of "outsiders" *in the name of the scriptural God!* In the classic cases of South Africa and North America, the scriptural phraseology of "Canaanites" was actually used to speak of the inhabitants of the land in order to justify the takeover of that land *in the name of the scriptural God!* What is stunning in this regard is that the Europeans who perpetrated such extreme acts of atrocity would have been themselves considered as "Gentiles" or "Hellenes," and by extension "Canaanites," by Paul and his followers, as is evident in the Gospels: the "Greek (*Hellinis*; Hellene) Syrophoenician" woman in Mark (7:26) becomes "Canaanite" in Matthew (15:22). In his letter to the patricians of Rome, mistress of the Roman empire (*oikoumenē*; habitation), Paul made sure to convey unequivocally the message that the Greco-Roman arrogant division of humankind between Hellenes (Greeks) and barbarians was untenable scripturally speaking; scripture lumps under the term "nations" (Hebrew *goyim*, Greek *ethnē*), without any kind of differentiation, all those who are not part of the *ekklēsia* of Israel:

> I want you to know, brethren, that I have often intended to come to you (but thus far have been prevented), in order that I may reap some harvest among you as well as among the rest of the Gentiles. I am under obligation both to Greeks (*Hellēsin*) and to barbarians, both to the wise and to the foolish: so I am eager to preach the gospel to you also who are in Rome. (Rom 1:13-15)

Yet, three centuries later during the post-Constantine era, the same Romans, now Christians, not only disregarded the message of the Apostle to the nations but even appealed to the cross, the symbol of his "gospel of peace," as a help in their warfare against the "barbarians":

> Save, O Lord, your people and bless you inheritance, granting victories (in the plural) to the kings (emperors) over (against) barbarians, and preserve, through the Cross, your commonwealth (*politevma*).

Even John Chrysostom, the Roman, fell prey to this fad of the times, which the post-Constantine era brought about.[5] The Crusaders, bearers of the "sign of the cross," were soon to follow suit. And, in our own days, the atrocities triggered as well as perpetrated by political Zionism are the latest version of a blatant mishearing of scripture.

Against this contemporary aberration a "scriptural" commentary on Joshua is not only welcome, but also necessary as well as timely.

---

[5] In his commentary on Isaiah he actualizes Is 2:2-4 about universal peace in terms of the pax Romana (Roman peace): "In addition to that, there is now much peace throughout the world. Even if there are a few wars, it is not like it was before. Back then, cities fought against cities, countries against countries, and races against races, and a single nation would be broken into many parts ... And this not the only difficulty. The law commanded that all the men bear arms, and no one was immune of this service. This law was enforced not only among the Jews, but throughout the world ... Since the sun of righteousness began to shine, and all cities and peoples and nations have received so much life from these commandments, they do not know how to engage wars ... Even if there are a few wars now, they are at the borders of Roman rule and are not between cities and countries as before ... Consider how all these cities enjoy complete tranquility; they learn of war by rumor alone. Of course Christ could have taken away what is left of warfare, but for the sake of correction to the lazy, who become more frivolous under constant peace, he allows the barbarian [my emphasis] raids. And, to those who can correctly understand it, the prophet has indicated that wars would no longer be so frequent. He did not say, 'There shall no longer be any wars whatsoever,' but 'And nation shall not lift up the sword against nation.' He also speaks of the freedom the general populace enjoys: 'They shall not train for war,' with the exception of a few soldiers regimented for that purpose." In Duane A. Garrett, *An Analysis of the Hermeneutics of John Chrysostom's Commentary on Isaiah 1-8 with an English Translation.*; Lampeter, Wales: Edwin Mellen Press; 1992, pp.70-71.

1

Call and Mission of Joshua

Moses and Joshua

Joshua 1:1-9 serves as an introduction and sets the tone for the entire book by positing it as a hinge between the Law and the Prophets. On the one hand, we hear of the divine oath to the fathers in Genesis (v.6) as well as the promise to Moses (v.3) in the following books of the Torah concerning the inheritance of the "earth" the Israelites are invited to receive under Joshua's leadership. On the other hand, beginning with Judges and up to the end of 2 Kings (The Prior Prophets), we hear of the stubborn disobedience of the Israelites, disobedience that cost them that inheritance. Besides underscoring again the multi-faceted disregard of God's law, the Latter Prophets function as reminder that "turning to the Lord" in obedience will vouchsafe the implementation of God's promise concerning that "earth" where all its "families" will live together securely under his blessing, as promised to Abraham (Gen 12:2-3). Since Joshua 1:1-9 "announces" the compendium of the entire message of the book, it would behoove us to delve into it in detail.

The book opens with "After the death of Moses, the servant of the Lord, the Lord said to Joshua the son of Nun, Moses' minister" (Josh 1:1). The most striking feature of this statement is the different titles given to Moses and Joshua. Moses is identified as "the servant of the Lord," which is a staple of the book.[1] Joshua, on the other hand, is connected to the Lord through Moses and thus is secondary; he is merely Moses'

---

[1] 1:1, 2, 7, 13, 15; 8:31, 33; 9:24; 11:12, 15; 12:6; 13:8; 14:7; 18:7; 22:2, 4, 5.

31

minister. To be sure, later we will hear of Joshua as "servant": "When Joshua was by Jericho, he lifted up his eyes and looked, and behold, a man stood before him with his drawn sword in his hand; and Joshua went to him and said to him, 'Are you for us, or for our adversaries?' And he said, 'No; but as commander of the army of the Lord I have now come.' And Joshua fell on his face to the earth, and worshiped, and said to him, 'What does my lord bid his servant?'" (5:13-14). Yet even though we hear of Joshua as servant, when compared with the references to Moses, two major differences are evident: (1) it is Joshua who introduces himself as "servant" whereas Moses is systematically introduced by the author as such because it is God himself who bestows that title on him (1:2), and (2) Joshua is just the servant of the "commander of the army of the Lord." It is only at his death in the closing chapter of the book that Joshua is granted the title of "servant of the Lord" (24:29). During his lifetime he is consistently Moses' minister (*mešaret*) as is evident also from Exodus 24:13; 33:11[2] and Numbers 11:28. Consequently, Joshua is subservient to Moses or, more specifically, to the Law that Moses embodies. Indeed, the book opens with the mention of the death of Moses only to immediately introduce God's lengthy injunction to Joshua during which he is summoned to be "careful to do according to all the law which Moses my servant commanded you" (Josh 1:7a). More explicitly, this law is said to be "this book of the law … that you may be careful to do according to all that is written in it" (v.8). This book of the law is the Book of Deuteronomy (29:21; 30:10; 31:26) that is addressed to the new generation (1:35-36; 5:1-3). Joshua will not only have to circumcise (Josh 5:2-9) this new generation, but also will have to read to them the Law of Deuteronomy

---

[2] In these two instances RSV unwarrantedly translates *mešaret* into "servant."

(compare Josh 8:32-35 with Deut 11:26-32). A further indication that supports the link between Joshua and Deuteronomy is that the phrase "be strong and of good courage," which is found thrice on God's lips (Josh 1:6, 7, 9), occurs in Moses' last words to Joshua (Deut 31:23) just before the last mention of "this book of the law" (vv.24-26): "When Moses had finished writing the words of this law in a book, to the very end, Moses commanded the Levites who carried the ark of the covenant of the Lord, 'Take this book of the law, and put it by the side of the ark of the covenant of the Lord your God, that it may be there for a witness against you.'" Put otherwise, Moses the man died in order that Moses the book, and through it God himself, might remain as the sure guide for the following generations. In the Law it is Moses who refers to God, in the Prophets it is God who refers to Moses! Notice how, although Moses' death is already mentioned at the beginning of Joshua (v.1), God's injunction starts with the assertive "Moses my servant is dead" (v.2a) to introduce the divine command to Joshua (v.2b). That the beginning of Joshua harks back unambiguously to Deuteronomy is again evident in the closeness in terminology:

> Every place on which the sole of your foot treads shall be yours; your territory shall be from the wilderness and Lebanon and from the River, the river Euphrates, to the western sea. No man shall be able to stand against you. (Deut 11:24-25a)

> Every place that the sole of your foot will tread upon I have given to you, as I promised to Moses. From the wilderness and this Lebanon as far as the great river, the river Euphrates, all the land of the Hittites to the Great Sea toward the going down of the sun shall be your territory. No man shall be able to stand before you all the days of your life. (Josh 1:3-5a)

When one compares these two descriptions of the earth granted to "the children of Israel" (Josh 1:2)[3] one cannot avoid being struck by the addition "all the land of the Hittites" in Joshua. This seemed strange even to the LXX translators who eliminated it. The obvious aim of the addition is to stretch the area of the earth in order to make it impossible to circumscribe unless one is speaking of an empire. However, since in scripture earthly kingship is an abomination against the sole King of Israel, the Lord himself, the intention behind this addition must be sought elsewhere. When one hears the Book of Joshua within the full range of the Prophets, then one will understand that Canaan refers to a vast expanse of pasture land for tribes of shepherds to enjoy and, in fact, such tribes still do so in the contemporary Near East.[4] This view fits perfectly with Ezekiel's anti-kingly teaching that culminates with "the earth of Israel" (*'ereṣ yisra'el*) being transformed into "the ground of Israel" (*'admat yisra'el*), that is, an earth for every human being (*'adam*), just as a pasture is open grazing for any and all sheep that happen to be on it.[5] In Ezekiel 34, the King of Israel becomes its shepherd[6] and his elect one, King David, is demoted to prince, and then becomes a shepherd to his subjects (Ezek 34:23-24; 37:24-25; see also Jer 3:15).[7] So it is against this background that one can understand the function of the addition "all the land of the Hittites" (Josh 1:3). It is Ephron *the Hittite* who invited the shepherd Abraham to realize that God's blessing would not materialize as a true blessing unless it is shared by all "the

---

[3] RSV has "the people of Israel" for the Hebrew *bene yisra'el*.

[4] See Gen 13:14b-15: "Lift up your eyes, and look from the place where you are, northward and southward and eastward and westward; for *all the land (earth) which you see* I will give to you and to your descendants for ever."

[5] See *C-Ezek* 114-7; 171-2; 186-9; 324.

[6] See also Is 40:7.

[7] See my comments in *C-Ezek* 146-7; 229; 312.

families of (God's) earth."[8] Indeed, the first foothold of Abraham,[9] the father of Israel, in the earth of God's promise was secured by God through Ephron the Hittite who generously offered to share his field with Abraham forever (Gen 22). Allowing someone to have a family burial place on one's ground is a long-term commitment: the place of Sarah's burial will also be that of Isaac (35:29), Rebecca and Leah (49:31), and Jacob (49:28-30; 50:12-13) as well as that of Abraham himself (25:9-10). At the final restoration, Zion, the new Jerusalem, will be cast as the progeny of Abraham and the barren Sarah and, very à propos, likened to a tent, a shepherd's abode (Is 51:1-2; 54:1-2).[10] The priority of Abraham over Moses in the matter of the gift of the earth is evident in that although the first mention of that gift is made through Moses (Josh 1:3), starting with v.6 it is the "fathers" who are repeatedly introduced as the recipients of that promise (1:6; 5:6; 21:43, 44). In all those instances we hear that God committed himself with an oath, whereas he simply "said" it to Moses (1:3).[11] The priority of the fathers over Moses is manifest in the pericopes of Moses' call:

---

[8] See my comments on Gen 23 in *LAC* 71-4.

[9] Notice the repeated reference to a tent as his abode (Gen 12:8; 13:3, 5, 12, 18; 18:1, 2, 6, 9, 10).

[10] It is worth noting that in Is 54:5-6 the new Zion is spoken of as God's wife: "For your Maker is your husband, the Lord of hosts is his name; and the Holy One of Israel is your Redeemer, the God of the whole earth he is called. For the Lord has called you like a wife forsaken and grieved in spirit, like a wife of youth when she is cast off, says your God." This fits perfectly with what we hear in Genesis regarding Isaac being the outcome of the Lord's promise to Sarah (Gen 17:21; see also Gal 4:23). The same imagery is used in Gen 4:1 to speak of Cain, the first "child" in scripture, as having been "gotten" by Eve "with the Lord" (*'et yahweh*); the RSV's explicative addition "the help of" is not in the original.

[11] RSV erroneously has "promised" for the Hebrew *dibbarti* ([I] said, spoke). Both KJV and JB translate it into "I said."

And he [the Lord] said, "I am the God of your father, the God of Abraham, the God of Isaac, and the God of Jacob." And Moses hid his face, for he was afraid to look at God. Then the Lord said, "I have seen the affliction of my people who are in Egypt, and have heard their cry because of their taskmasters; I know their sufferings, and I have come down to deliver them out of the hand of the Egyptians, and to bring them up out of that land to a good and broad land, a land flowing with milk and honey, to the place of the Canaanites, the Hittites, the Amorites, the Perizzites, the Hivites, and the Jebusites" ... Then Moses said to God, "If I come to the people of Israel and say to them, 'The God of your fathers has sent me to you,' and they ask me, 'What is his name?' what shall I say to them?" God said to Moses, "I am who I am." And he said, "Say this to the people of Israel, 'I am has sent me to you.'" God also said to Moses, "Say this to the people of Israel, 'The Lord, the God of your fathers, the God of Abraham, the God of Isaac, and the God of Jacob, has sent me to you': this is my name for ever, and thus I am to be remembered throughout all generations. Go and gather the elders of Israel together, and say to them, 'The Lord, the God of your fathers, the God of Abraham, of Isaac, and of Jacob, has appeared to me, saying, I have observed you and what has been done to you in Egypt.'" (Ex 3:6-8, 13-16)

And God said to Moses, "I am the Lord. I appeared to Abraham, to Isaac, and to Jacob, as God Almighty, but by my name the Lord I did not make myself known to them. I also established my covenant with them, to give them the land of Canaan, the land in which they dwelt as sojourners. Moreover I have heard the groaning of the people of Israel whom the Egyptians hold in bondage and I have remembered my covenant. Say therefore to the people of Israel, 'I am the Lord, and I will bring you out from under the burdens of the Egyptians, and I will deliver you from their bondage, and I will redeem you with an outstretched arm and with great acts of judgment, and I will take you for my people, and I will be your God; and you shall know that I am the

Lord your God, who has brought you out from under the burdens
of the Egyptians. And I will bring you into the land which I swore
to give to Abraham, to Isaac, and to Jacob; I will give it to you for
a possession. I am the Lord.'" (6:2-8)

The Prominence of the Law

So what is the function of Moses and why is the Law given the
place of eminence in Joshua? Besides the reference three times to
Moses at the outset (Josh 1:3), strict adherence to the Law is
presented as a condition for the implementation of God's
promise to the fathers:

> Be strong and of good courage (*ḥazaq we'emaṣ*); for you shall cause
> this people to inherit the land which I swore to their fathers to
> give them. Only (*raq*) be strong and very courageous (*ḥazaq
> we'emaṣ*), being careful to do according to all the law which Moses
> my servant commanded you; turn not from it to the right hand or
> to the left, that you may have good success wherever you go. This
> book of the law shall not depart out of your mouth, but you shall
> meditate on it day and night, that you may be careful to do
> according to all that is written in it; for then you shall make your
> way prosperous, and then you shall have good success. Have I not
> commanded you? Be strong and of good courage; be not
> frightened, neither be dismayed; for the Lord your God is with
> you wherever you go. (Josh 1:6-9)

Since the same *ḥazaq we'emaṣ* (Be strong and of good courage) in
v.6 is immediately recalled verbatim in Hebrew in v.7 with the
caveat *raq* (only), it ensues that the gift of "an earth flowing with
milk and honey" (5:6) is not unconditional.[12] The condition is
that Joshua strictly abide by "*all* that is written in the book of the
law." The seriousness of this caveat is evident in its repetition

---

[12] The same was the case with Adam and the garden in Eden (Gen 2).

over two verses. This passage presents us with several particularities. First, it is curious, to say the least, that the "success" of the settlement in the earth of the promise is contingent solely on Joshua's obedience to the Law. To be sure, later the same Law will be read aloud to the entire people (8:32-35), however, there is no mention of a condition similar to that imposed on Joshua. The solution to this apparent conundrum lies in understanding that the Books of Joshua and Judges function as a diptych: both deal with the same period of settlement but each from a different perspective.[13] Joshua underscores that the earth is a gift from the Lord to the people; Judges prepares for the lengthy story ending with 2 Kings that relates how the people and their leaders reneged on the Lord and, in so doing, forfeited that gift. Indeed, the discrepancy between the differing attitudes of the people, before and after Joshua's death, straddles the two books:

> After these things Joshua the son of Nun, the servant of the Lord, died, being a hundred and ten years old. And they buried him in his own inheritance at Timnathserah, which is in the hill country of Ephraim, north of the mountain of Gaash. And Israel served the Lord all the days of Joshua, and all the days of the elders who outlived Joshua and had known all the work which the Lord did for Israel. (Josh 24:29-31)

> When Joshua dismissed the people, the people of Israel went each to his inheritance to take possession of the land. And the people served the Lord all the days of Joshua, and all the days of the elders who outlived Joshua, who had seen all the great work which the Lord had done for Israel. And Joshua the son of Nun, the servant of the Lord, died at the age of one hundred and ten years. And they buried him within the bounds of his inheritance in

---

[13] See further on this matter *OTI* 143-57.

Timnathheres, in the hill country of Ephraim, north of the mountain of Gaash. And all that generation also were gathered to their fathers; and there arose another generation after them, who did not know the Lord or the work which he had done for Israel. And the people of Israel did what was evil in the sight of the Lord and served the Baals; and they forsook the Lord, the God of their fathers, who had brought them out of the land of Egypt; they went after other gods, from among the gods of the peoples who were round about them, and bowed down to them; and they provoked the Lord to anger. They forsook the Lord, and served the Baals and the Ashtaroth. (Judg 2:6-13)

Thus, unlike Moses who was not able to protect his generation during the trek through the wilderness, Joshua proved to be, as his name indicates, the "savior" of his contemporaries. Although he started his mission as "Moses' minister" (Josh 1:1b), he proved at the end to be as much "the servant of the Lord" (24:29) as Moses (1:1a). In a way he surpassed Moses since he is described as being fully obedient to God and, as a result, was granted to settle his people in the earth of promise. Due to his disobedience, Moses was barred from crossing into that earth (Deut 32:48-52). The special value bestowed on Joshua as the implementer of God's salvation in spite of the people's obduracy had been prepared for at his first mention in scripture:

All the congregation of the people of Israel moved on from the wilderness of Sin by stages, according to the commandment of the Lord, and camped at Rephidim; but there was no water for the people to drink. Therefore the people found fault with Moses, and said, "Give us water to drink." And Moses said to them, "Why do you find fault with me? Why do you put the Lord to the proof?" But the people thirsted there for water, and the people murmured against Moses, and said, "Why did you bring us up out of Egypt, to kill us and our children and our cattle with thirst?" So Moses cried to the Lord, "What shall I do with this people? They are almost ready to stone me." And the Lord said to Moses, "Pass on before the people, taking with you some of the elders of Israel; and take in your hand the rod with which you struck the Nile, and go. Behold, I will stand before you there on the rock at Horeb; and you shall strike the rock, and water shall come out of it, that the people may drink." And Moses did so, in the sight of the elders of Israel. And he called the name of the place Massah and Meribah, because of the faultfinding of the children of Israel, and because they put the Lord to the proof by saying, "Is the Lord among us or not?" Then came Amalek and fought with Israel at Rephidim. And Moses said to Joshua, "Choose for us men, and go out, fight with Amalek; tomorrow I will stand on the top of the hill with the rod of God in my hand." So Joshua did as Moses told him, and fought with Amalek; and Moses, Aaron, and Hur went up to the top of the hill. Whenever Moses held up his hand, Israel prevailed; and whenever he lowered his hand, Amalek prevailed. But Moses' hands grew weary; so they took a stone and put it under him, and he sat upon it, and Aaron and Hur held up his hands, one on one side, and the other on the other side; so his hands were steady until the going down of the sun.[14] And Joshua mowed down Amalek and his people with the edge of the sword. (Ex 17:1-13)

That the scriptural Joshua is the major "component" that holds the Law and the Prophets together can be detected also in that the names of the first book of the Prior Prophets (Joshua), the first book of the Latter Prophets (Isaiah), and the first book of the Scroll of the Twelve Prophets (Hosea) are from the same root _yšʿ_ that has the connotation of salvation; moreover in the first two cases the names include the root _yh_ that is a shortened form of _yhwh_ (the Lord). The Prior Prophets tell the story of the people who were punished due to their disobedience to the Law. The Latter Prophets enhance this and then offer a second chance leading to salvation to the following generations who are to live

---

[14] Notice how this looks ahead to Josh 10:12-13.

according to that same Law. Thus the Book of Joshua, through its scriptural main character, is the hinge that holds together the entire scriptural story as the "conditional" story of God's salvation.[15]

The arrangement of Isaiah and the Twelve Prophets seems to be intentional. Looking at the structure of the Latter Prophets (Isaiah, Jeremiah, Ezekiel, the Twelve Prophets) one notices that they form an *inclusio*: ABB'A'. While the two central books revolve around the fall of Jerusalem to the Babylonians, the first and the last are conceived as a story line, just as in the Prior Prophets. Indeed, Isaiah (*yeša'yahu*, the Lord will save) and the Twelve Prophets, beginning with Hosea (*hošea'*, [the Lord] has brought salvation) and ending with Malachi (*mal'aki*, my messenger), take us from the time of Samaria's sin, to Jerusalem's sin and the exile, then to the ultimate coming of the Lord to judge (condemn the unrighteous and save the humble). On the other hand, looking at both the Prior and the Latter Prophets, one cannot miss that the names Joshua and Hosea also bracket that entire scriptural section forming the *inclusio*. In other words, the name of Joshua could well stand for "the Prophets" in the same way that the name Moses stands for "the Law." This is hinted at, if not outright supported, by the text itself. Whereas in Exodus we systematically hear of *yehošua'* (Joshua; Ex 17:9, 10, 13, 14; 24:13; 32:17; 33:11), this same person is suddenly introduced as *hošea'* (Hosea) in both Numbers and Deuteronomy. That we are dealing with the same individual is beyond any doubt. In Numbers, where we find the continuation of the story started in Exodus, one again encounters *yehošua'*

---

[15] In Rom 6 Paul clearly teaches that divine grace is a second chance to follow the divine bidding.

(Joshua; Num 11:28). However, two chapters later one hears the
following:

> The Lord said to Moses, "Send men to spy out the land of
> Canaan, which I give to the people of Israel; from each tribe of
> their fathers shall you send a man, every one a leader among
> them." So Moses sent them from the wilderness of Paran,
> according to the command of the Lord, all of them men who were
> heads of the people of Israel. And these were their names: From
> the tribe of Reuben, Shammua the son of Zaccur; from the tribe
> of Simeon, Shaphat the son of Hori; from the tribe of Judah,
> Caleb the son of Jephunneh; from the tribe of Issachar, Igal the
> son of Joseph; from the tribe of Ephraim, *Hoshea* (hošea') *the son
> of Nun*; from the tribe of Benjamin, Palti the son of Raphu; from
> the tribe of Zebulun, Gaddiel the son of Sodi; from the tribe of
> Joseph (that is from the tribe of Manasseh), Gaddi the son of Susi;
> from the tribe of Dan, Ammiel the son of Gemalli; from the tribe
> of Asher, Sethur the son of Michael; from the tribe of Naphtali,
> Nahbi the son of Vophsi; from the tribe of Gad, Geuel the son of
> Machi. These were the names of the men whom Moses sent to spy
> out the land. *And Moses called Hoshea* (hošea') *the son of Nun
> Joshua* (yehošua'). (13:1-16)

Then, as if he wanted the hearers to realize that this was not a
passing thought on his part, at the conclusion of the entire
Pentateuchal story the author writes: "Moses came and recited all
the words of this song in the hearing of the people, he and
Hoshea (hošea') *the son of Nun*."[16] (Deut 32:44) So, already in the
Law, we find the blue print of the connection Joshua-Hosea. In
turn, this literary device seals the interconnection between the
Prophets and the Law, more specifically, Deuteronomy, the
Book of the Law.

---

[16] Correctly so in KJV; RSV and JB have "Joshua" instead.

Still the consonantal Hebrew for Joshua is יְהוֹשֻׁעַ that transliterates as *yhoš'* or *yhwš'*.[17] Since the rule in Hebrew is that a final accented syllable requires a long vowel, one would have expected יְהוֹשֵׁעַ (*yehošea'*) just as in הוֹשֵׁעַ (*hošea'*), the name of the prophet Hosea, with the prefix *yh* the shortened form of *yhwh* (the Lord). The alternative would be to have lengthened the short vowel *u* into the long *û*, but that would have required to add the consonant ו (*w*) after the שׁ (*š*) and transform יְהוֹשֻׁעַ into יְהוֹשׁוּעַ which is precisely how Joshua is referred to in both Deuteronomy 3:21 and Judges 2:7. The conclusion is obvious: the author wanted to allude to another verbal form while preserving the connection Joshua-Hosea. That other verbal form שׁוּעַ (*šua'*) has the connotation of "cry for help," which would give to יְהוֹשׁוּעַ (Joshua) the meaning of "the Lord is (the object of) our cry for help."[18] This seems to fit the function of Joshua perfectly. Victory leading to salvation, which is reflected in the root *yš'* found in the names of Isaiah and Hosea, is the prerogative of a military leader. However, in spite of all that is misguidedly yet commonly said of Joshua, he is definitely not a military leader as is evident in the following dialogue just before the fall of Jericho:

> When Joshua was by Jericho, he lifted up his eyes and looked, and behold, a man stood before him with his drawn sword in his hand; and Joshua went to him and said to him, "Are you for us, or for our adversaries?" And he said, "No; but as commander (*śar*) of the army of the Lord I have now come." And Joshua fell on his face to the earth, and worshiped, and said to him, "What does my lord bid his servant?" And the commander (*śar*) of the Lord's army said

---

[17] In Hebrew the transliterated consonants *o* and *w* are the same letter ו.

[18] I am indebted to my colleague Iskandar Abou-Chaar from Lebanon for this insight.

to Joshua, "Put off your shoes from your feet; for the place where you stand is holy." And Joshua did so. (Josh 5:13-15)

When one takes into consideration the profuse use of "king" and "kings" to speak of the leaders of the Canaanite cities, one is surprised to hear that the Israelites have only a commander who is not even Joshua himself. Such aversion against kingship will become more pronounced in the following Books of Judges, Samuel, and Kings in preparation for the declaration in the Latter Prophets that God alone is the sole King of Israel. On the other hand, and more à propos, would be to question how Joshua could have been an actual military commander when he was supposed to abide by the divine injunction that "this book of the law shall not depart out of your mouth, but you shall meditate on it day and night, that you may be careful to do according to all that is written in it," especially since his success depended on such behavior (1:8). Consequently, it is Joshua's strict obedience to the Law that will preserve the people. After his death, the same people will opt for having a king (1 Sam 8) and, in spite of all appearances under David and Solomon, by doing so, they will be doomed to eventual destruction and exile.

Inheritance and Possession

Those who view the Book of Joshua as relaying the conquest of Canaan by cunning, let alone by force, are led astray by misguided translations. More often than not such translations reflect the subconscious wishes or preferences of the translators. The most flagrant misreading is the repeated rendering of the original "inherit" and "inheritance" into "possess" and "possession," beginning with Joshua 1. Compare the following:

Hebrew MT

⁶Be strong and of good courage; for you shall *cause* this people *to inherit (tanḥil)* the earth which I swore to their fathers to give them.

¹¹Pass through the camp, and command the people, "Prepare your provisions; for within three days you are to pass over this Jordan, to go in *to inherit (larešet)* the earth which the Lord your God gives you *to inherit it (larištah)*."

¹⁵until the Lord gives rest to your brethren as well as to you, *and they* also *inherit (weyarešu)* the land which the Lord your God is giving them; then you shall return to the earth *of your inheritance (yeruššatkem), and shall inherit (wyrištem)* it, which Moses the servant of the Lord gave you beyond the Jordan toward the sunrise.

LXX

⁶Be strong and of good courage; for you shall *allot (apodiasteleis; divide)* to this people the earth which I swore to their fathers to give them.

¹¹Pass through the camp, and command the people, "Prepare your provisions; for within three days you are to pass over this Jordan, to go in to *hold unto (kataskhein)* the earth which the God of your fathers gives you."

¹⁵until the Lord gives rest to your brethren as well as to you, and they also *inherit (klēronomēsōsin)* the land which the Lord your God is giving them; then you shall return each to his *inheritance (klēronomian)* which Moses the servant of the Lord gave you beyond the Jordan toward the sunrise.

KJV

[6] Be strong and of a good courage: for unto this people shalt thou *divide for an inheritance* the land, which I sware unto their fathers to give them.

[11]Pass through the host, and command the people, saying, Prepare you victuals; for within three days ye shall pass over this Jordan, to go in to *possess* the land, which the Lord your God giveth you to *possess* it.

[15]Until the Lord have given your brethren rest, as *he hath given*[19] you, and they also have *possessed* the land which the Lord your God giveth them: then ye shall return unto the land of your *possession*, and enjoy it, which Moses the Lord's servant gave you on this side Jordan toward the sunrising.

JB

[6]Be strong and stand firm, for you are the man to *give* this people *possession* of the land which I swore to their ancestors that I would give them.

[11]Go through the camp and give the people this order, "Make provisions ready, for in three days' time you will cross this Jordan and go on to *take possession* of the land which Yahweh your God is giving you as your own."

[15]until Yahweh grants rest to your brothers and you alike, when they too have *taken possession* of the land which Yahweh your God is giving to them. Then you may go back and *take possession* of the land which *belongs to you* and which Moses, servant of Yahweh, has given you on the eastern side of the Jordan.

---

[19] This italicization is in the original.

RSV

[6]Be strong and of good courage; for you shall *cause* this people *to inherit* the land which I swore to their fathers to give them.

[11]Pass through the camp, and command the people, "Prepare your provisions; for within three days you are to pass over this Jordan, to go in to *take possession* of the land which the Lord your God gives you *to possess.*"

[15]until the Lord gives rest to your brethren as well as to you, and they also *take possession* of the land which the Lord your God is giving them; then you shall return to the land *of your possession*, and shall *possess* it, the land which Moses the servant of the Lord gave you beyond the Jordan toward the sunrise.

Even a cursory glance at the different translations will readily show a predilection for "possession" over "inheritance." The most surprising aspect is that even the KJV, which is usually a more accurate translation, takes the liberty to render both the Hebrew *yaraš* and the Greek *klēronom*—, which are technical terms reflecting inheritance, into "possess" and "possession" in v.15. What may have led the way toward such an error is the LXX's rendering of *yaraš* into *kataskhein* (hold unto) instead of *klēronomein* (inheritance) in v.11. Still, the LXX is the most seasoned among translations. Its "intelligent" choice of vocabulary follows a consistent pattern; however, one would have to study its use of words just as one must do with the Hebrew original. So it is important to try to understand the "inheritance" phraseology of Joshua in both the MT and the LXX in order to actually realize what the author is saying regarding Canaan as the earth of the promise.

Possession reflects personal ownership of property. Students of the European Middle Ages are familiar with manors. The manor was the landed property of the knight or lord who had absolute ownership and authority over both it and the residents who enjoyed and lived out of that land but who never owned any of it. An inheritance, especially one that is a patrimony, conveys land as a family estate bequeathed by the father to whomever he *chooses*, while it remains always a *family* estate. In scripture, the sacredness and inalienability of the patrimony is reflected in the story of Naboth's vineyard (1 Kg 21).

As its Latin original *patrimonium* indicates, a patrimony is a reminder (forewarning)[20] by the father and, by the same token, a remembrance of him. Consequently, the only person who can manage the patrimony is the heir assigned by that father.[21] Once in charge, the heir becomes the paterfamilias who, in turn, assigns his own heir, or designates the heir according to the directives of the original paterfamilias. Thus the assignment is always the prerogative of the "father," and this is precisely why the family estate remains a *patri*mony. The oneness of the heir in every subsequent generation insures the preemption of any tension regarding the patrimony, a tension that would be a predicament in the case of multiple heirs. Since a monarch is the "father" of the kingdom's citizens, he is the manager of his family's patrimony, which amounts to his realm. In Semitic languages, this reality is mirrored in the name *melek* by which the monarch is known, the literal meaning of which is owner or proprietor. His realm as well as his status is either *malkut* or *mamlakah* from the same root *mlk*. The similar situation is found in European countries. A king manages a kingdom or a realm, the latter taken from the Latin *regimen* through the French *royaume*, which derive from the Latin *rex* (king) and the

---

[20] The Latin verb *moneo* is still distinguishable in the English "admonish."
[21] Paul refers to this rule in Gal 4:1-2.

French *roi* (king). Because the king is the sole proprietor of the realm, his "children" are also his "subjects" just as in the Roman household the children as well as the slaves are equally members of the paterfamilias' household and are *subject* to his will. The patrimony was essential in preserving the perpetuity of kingdoms through royal dynasties, whether genetically or by adoption. Ancient kingdoms, however, often underwent upheavals that brought about new dynasties. When this happened, the kingdom's main deity, who functioned as its "parent," insured the perpetuity of the patrimony. It was precisely the oneness of that parent that bridged the gap between one dynasty and another; in essence, all monarchs were equally "sons of (their) god" by assignment (see 1 Sam 12:13; 16:8-12; Ps 2:6-8). Consequently, even in the most autocratic dynasties, the patrimony was secure because it lay in the good will of the one deity whose parenthood spanned decades and centuries. In the truest sense, only the deity was the parent of the citizens, albeit through the agency of the monarch. The deity alone allowed the monarch as well as the people to reside in its realm *as an inheritance*, never as their own property.

Scripture's peculiarity, if not uniqueness, is that it presents *all* the kings in a negative light in order to heighten the absolute kingship of God. The Book of Joshua pushes this stand to its extreme. In the following books of the Prior Prophets (Judges, Samuel, and Kings) one does hear of kings of Israel and Judah; in Joshua, however, reference to kings is confined to the Canaanite cities. The Israelites have no king! It is the scriptural proclivity to extremism that transforms a common tradition or story into a hyperbole rather than a simple parabole. Divine punishment followed by forgiveness is a staple of scripture. This theme is also heard in stories of other deities. In the prayer of

King Mesha of Moab inscribed on the Moabite Stone, discovered in Dhiban in Jordan in 1868, one hears such a story:

> I am Mesha, son of Chemosh, king of Moab, the Dibonite. My father ruled over Moab for thirty years, and I became king after my father. And I made this high place for Chemosh in Qarhoh. I built it as a sign of victory, for he saved me from all the kings and let me see my desire on all my enemies. Omri was king of Israel, and he oppressed Moab for a long time, *for Chemosh was angry with his land.* And his son succeeded him and he too said: 'I will oppress Moab.' In my days Chemosh spoke thus, and I looked down on him and on his throne. And it was Israel which perished for ever, although Omri had taken possession of the whole land of Madeba. And he dwelt in it during his days and half of the days of his son, forty years, but *Chemosh dwelt in it in my days.*[22]

When comparing this text with the Old Testament prophetic literature, one is struck by the difference between the punishment of Moab and the punishment of Judah. Mesha had lost only part of his territory and was still king. In the prophetic story we encounter the total destruction of the kingdom and the exiles cast within the realm of the conqueror with no hope of relief except in those same prophetic words. No king is around to utter words of thanksgiving to God, let alone words of consolation to his people.

It is precisely this kind of hyperbolic approach that one encounters in Joshua concerning kingship. The patrimony of the earth of promise in Canaan is both initiated and maintained by God himself, the sole King of Israel, who, in every generation, either reassigns the inheritance or revokes it at will. Many exegetes as well as others studying scripture misunderstand the

---

[22] E. Lipinski, *The Mesha Inscription,* in Walter Bayerlin, *Near Eastern Religious Texts Relating to the Old Testament,* Philadelphia, 1978, p.238-9.

perpetuity of God's "promise" for the perpetuity of the gift of the "earth" itself.[23] God's absolute supremacy over *his* patrimony (inheritance) can be unequivocally seen in the following features of the Law: (1) the generation that left Egypt, including Moses, perished in the wilderness and did not enter Canaan; (2) anyone who disobeys the Law's statutes is excised from the congregation of Israel. That is to say, the people as a totality do not have a monopoly over any part of God's earth and its fate, nor does any individual have any power of entitlement over his own membership in the divine congregation.[24]

The Importance of the Hebrew Text

Judeo-Christian Zionism and even most Western theology since Karl Barth's Commentary on Romans (1933) commit the error, if not the outright blasphemy, of assuming that God is bound by his "inheritance" rather than those receiving the inheritance being bound by God's will expressed in the Law: blessing *or* curse in and for every generation (Lev 25; Deut 28; Josh 8:30-35). This view has been all but obliterated by the frequent translation of the Hebrew roots *yrš* and *nḥl* into "possess" and "possession," especially in Joshua, thus giving the impression that, regardless of how they behave, the earth is the people's deeded property. Therefore, closely examining the original text is critical to understanding the entire book.

The seriousness of the matter not only concerns the contemporary situation in the Middle East where many people

---

[23] Cast in Pauline terms, a similar mistake is done when the exegetes as well as the Corinthians mistake the divine *charisma* (gift) for God's *kharis* (gracefulness; source of the gift); the latter is not exhausted or depleted by the former that is either bestowed or negated by God for every new generation.

[24] See 1 Cor 5:1-5 besides all the instances of excision (being "cut off") in the Law (e.g. Ex 12:15, 19; 30:33, 38; 31:14; Lev 7:20-27; 17:4-14).

are paying the price of misguided Judeo-Christian Zionism at all levels, but also, and more importantly, an incorrect understanding of scripture is tantamount to tampering with God's own words and message. The painful fact is that translations are mere translations and in no way scripture itself. Even the LXX, the most intelligent of all translations, is still just a translation. To put it bluntly, *only in its original language* "all scripture is inspired by God and profitable for teaching, for reproof, for correction, and for training in righteousness" (2 Tim 3:16). The reason is clearly given in the prologue to Ecclesiasticus (The Wisdom of Sirach):

> Whereas many great teachings have been given to us through the law and the prophets and the others that followed them, on account of which we should praise Israel for instruction and wisdom; and since it is necessary not only that the readers themselves should acquire understanding but also that those who love learning should be able to help the outsiders by both speaking and writing, my grandfather Jesus, after devoting himself especially to the reading of the law and the prophets and the other books of our fathers, and after acquiring considerable proficiency in them, was himself also led to write something pertaining to instruction and wisdom, in order that, by becoming conversant with this also, those who love learning should make even greater progress in living according to the law.

> You are urged therefore to read with good will and attention, and to be indulgent in cases where, despite our diligent labor in translating, we may seem to have rendered some phrases imperfectly. For what was originally expressed in Hebrew does not have exactly the same sense when translated into another language. Not only this work, but even the law itself, the prophecies, and the rest of the books differ not a little as originally expressed.

When I came to Egypt in the thirty-eighth year of the reign of Euergetes and stayed for some time, I found opportunity for no little instruction. It seemed highly necessary that I should myself devote some pains and labor to the translation of the following book, using in that period of time great watchfulness and skill in order to complete and publish the book for those living abroad who wished to gain learning, being prepared in character to live according to the law.

Traditional Judaism and, more so, Islam took this cautionary warning very seriously. Although the *qur'an* has been translated into many languages for the sake of the believers, the reading aloud of the *qur'an* is done exclusively in the original Arabic; thus the *'imam* is bound to know Arabic in order to "understand" what it is saying and convey its message to the members of his congregation in their own language. One may not, technically speaking, exegete a translation since any translation is the product of its translators. This is evidenced in that the Septuagint, the earliest Greek translation of the Old Testament, is named after the number of the translators (seventy) who, according to a tradition preserved in the second century B.C. "Letter of Aristeas to Philocrates," took part in that project. Even more recent translations of the Bible are commonly known by the name of their commissioner (e.g., King James Version), or their author (Luther Bible; Van Dyke Arabic; Cornilescu [Romanian] Version), or the place of origin or conception (Geneva Bible; Zurich Bible; Romanian Bible; Jerusalem Bible). There are two compelling reasons why one may not exegete a translation. First of all, any text contains wordplay that is essential to the text's intent; even the best of translations cannot render accurately all instances of wordplay. Readers are no doubt aware of the difficulty inherent in translating proverbs from their original language into another language. Secondly, and more importantly, whenever scripture refers to God's speaking, then God is speaking in the original language of the text. Actually, whatever applies to God also applies to all the characters in the scriptural story. Let me give two examples, one from each of the Testaments. Whatever the language Joseph and Moses used to speak with Pharaoh, or the language Moses used with his Midianite wife, the content of these conversations is relayed to us *in Hebrew*. Similarly, the New Testament was written *in Greek*, and even when reference is made to another language, or even if it surmises such, for instance, that Herod and Pilate conversed in Latin (Lk 23:12), the author always has in mind his Greek understanding hearers. This is at its clearest in Acts in conjunction with one of Paul's speeches where, although the author relays that the Apostle spoke *in Hebrew*, the author's addressees hear Paul *in Greek*:

> And when he had given him leave, Paul, standing on the steps, motioned with his hand to the people; and when there was a great hush, he spoke to them in the Hebrew language, saying [viz. in Greek]: "Brethren and fathers, hear the defense which I now make before you." And when they heard that he addressed them in the Hebrew language, they were the more quiet. And he said [viz. in Greek]: "I am a Jew, born at Tarsus in Cilicia, but brought up in this city at the feet of Gamaliel, educated according to the strict manner of the law of our fathers, being zealous for God as you all are this day." (21:40-21:3)[25]

---

[25] The much advertised Aramaic Matthew, whose existence has never been proven— just as the existence of the Document Q (allegedly containing original sayings of Jesus) has never been evidenced—is nothing other than a device conceived in order to remind the Greek hearers of the importance of the knowledge of Semitic languages. They ought to never forget that their New Testament relies on the LXX, which in turn relies on the original Hebrew. It is no coincidence that the tradition regarding an Aramaic Gospel was linked to Matthew, the Gospel that underscores the centrality of "the Law and the Prophets," which is typical Hebrew Old Testament terminology.

So this discussion of inheritance in Joshua will first deal with the Hebrew text and then investigate how the LXX handled the original. I shall limit myself to the LXX since it is the only Old Testament translation that preceded the rise of the New Testament writings and thus was not influenced by these. Subsequent translations of scripture do not share this place of honor with the LXX and, consequently, are irrelevant for understanding the Book of Joshua.

The speakers of modern languages use two voices to distinguish "I" verbal conjugation, the active—as in "I take"—and the passive—as in "I was taken." Those who know classical Greek are aware of a third voice, corresponding to our reflexive: doing something for one's own benefit.[26] In comparison, the versatility of Semitic languages is evidenced by the much larger number of verbal "forms" or "voices" for each triliteral verbal root. Hebrew has seven such verbal forms. The third and, especially, the fifth are known as "causative": to make (cause) someone else (to) do the action. To give an idea, the lengthy English "I make (cause) you (to) see a land" is rendered in Hebrew as two words: "I-make-you-see a-land" (*'ar'eka 'ereṣ*). Similarly, the English "*you shall cause* (this people) *to inherit* (the land)" (Josh 1:6) is in Hebrew simply the fifth verbal form *tanḥil* of the verb *naḥal* (receive as inheritance), inheritance being *naḥalah*.[27] The other root connoting inheritance is *yrš*: while *yaraš* means "[he] inherits," the fifth verbal form *horiš* means

---

[26] This voice is more readily heard in French than in English. The English "I wash my hands" sounds in French "I wash me the hands" (middle; reflexive) as opposed to "I wash him the hands" (active).

[27] While the fifth verbal form *hinḥil* (he caused to inherit) is the more common form, the third verbal form *niḥal*, being also causative, occurs in Josh 13:32; 14:1; and 19:51.

"[he] caused [someone] to inherit," *yerussah* being inheritance, heritage.[28]

Both roots *nhl* and *yrs* basically have the same meaning "inherit, receive as heritage," as witnessed in the LXX that translates both with the same Greek root *klēronom*— in Joshua. So it is stunning that even KJV, which is mimicked by RSV, opts for rendering the root *yrs* into "possess" and "possession," especially when one considers that it is precisely this root that is used in Genesis essentially in conjunction with Abraham, Isaac, and Jacob, each of whom are referred to at the beginning of Joshua as the recipients of the divine oath concerning the inheritance (1:6).[29] In so doing, these two English translations already, even if ingenuously, equate (common) heritage with (individual or communal) possession. As a result, the hearers who do not know Hebrew, or even Greek for that matter, are simply not hearing scripture but rather the translators' understanding of it! In this particular case, their understanding is directly affecting their view of the ultimate tangible setting of scripture itself, that is, "the earth and the fullness thereof" which is the subject matter of Genesis 1 and, by the same token, of the entire scripture.

The closest one gets to the idea of possession is in the use of the Hebrew root *'hz* whose connotation is "take" whence the verb *'ahaz* (take, grasp, take hold of) and the noun *'ahuzzah* (something taken, something in one's possession) rendered in the

---

[28] Another term is *morasah* not found in Joshua, but occurring in Exodus in conjunction with the same subject: "And I will bring you into the land which I swore to give to Abraham, to Isaac, and to Jacob; I will give it to you *for a possession* (*morasah*; inheritance, heritage). I am the Lord." (Ex 6:8; RSV) KJV is more accurate in rendering *morasah* as "for an heritage."

[29] See Gen 15:3, 4 [twice], 7, 8; 21:10; 22:7; Ex 3:4, 7-8.

LXX as *kataskhesis* (Josh 21:21, 41; 22:4, 9, 19 [twice]) from the verb *katekhō* (take, grasp, hold on to). However, what is of paramount importance is that (1) the Greek noun *kataskhesis* renders the Hebrew infinitive *rešet* (1:11) which is from the root *yrš* (inherit), and (2) the Greek verb *klēronomō* (inherit) is translated from the Hebrew *'aḥaz* in both Joshua 22:9 and 19, the same verses in which *kataskhesis* renders *'aḥuzzah*. The conclusion is unavoidable: "taking," on the part of Israel, is nothing other than "receiving (in heritage)" and is in no way a conquest by force. Such is corroborated in that, very often elsewhere in scripture, the Hebrew *'aḥaz* has the Greek *lambanō* (receive, take) as its counterpart in the LXX. An English speaking person should not be perplexed at such since the English verb "take" has often the meaning of "receive" in phrases the like of "Please take the cake I am giving (offering) you." This is precisely what one hears later in Joshua: "But the fields of the city and its villages *had been given* (Hebrew *natenu*; Greek *edōken*) to Caleb the son of Jephunneh as his possession (Hebrew *'aḥuzzah*; Greek *kataskhesis*)" (21:12); "And now the Lord your God has given rest to your brethren, as he promised them; therefore turn and go to your home in the land where your possession (Hebrew *'aḥuzzah*; Greek *kataskhesis*) lies, which Moses the servant of the Lord *gave* (Hebrew *natan*; Greek *edōken*) you on the other side of the Jordan." (22:4) One hears outright that what Moses *gives* is the inheritance (*naḥalah*) that certain tribes *receive*, a rendering of the Hebrew verb *laqaḥ* whose exclusive meaning is "receive":

> With the other half of the tribe of Manasseh, the Reubenites and the Gadites received (*laqeḥu*) their inheritance (*naḥalah*), which Moses *gave* them, beyond the Jordan eastward, as Moses the servant of the Lord *gave* them. (13:8)

The Levites have no portion (Hebrew *ḥeleq*; Greek *meris*) among you, for the priesthood of the Lord is their heritage (Hebrew *naḥalah*; Greek *meris*); and Gad and Reuben and half the tribe of Manasseh have received (Hebrew *laqeḥu*; Greek *elabosan* from the verb *lambanō*) their inheritance (*naḥalah*) beyond the Jordan eastward, which Moses the servant of the Lord *gave* them. (18:7)

The last verse actually presents us with two features that round up as well as corroborate these findings. On the one hand, the LXX translation of the Hebrew *laqaḥ* into the Greek *lambanō*, a verb that also means "take," confirms the equivalence between *'aḥaz* (take) and *laqaḥ* (receive). Its corollary is that *'aḥuzzah* does not necessarily mean possession by force. On the other hand, that the LXX uses in the one verse the same *meris* to render both *ḥeleq* (portion) and *naḥalah* (inheritance) also underscores that the earth was granted by apportioning or allotment as is further evidenced in the other instances where the verb *ḥalaq* (apportion; divide) occurs (Josh 13:7; 14:5; 18:2, 5, 10; 19:51).

Looking more closely at these occurrences, one notices that, whereas in 14:5 and 18:10 it is the earth (*'ereṣ*; the land in RSV) that is apportioned, in the other four instances it is actually the *naḥalah* that is allotted. It would behoove us to review in detail the lengthy passage 18:1-10 since not only does it contain three of the six just mentioned instances (vv.2, 5, and 10) but it also includes v.7 referred to earlier:

Then the whole congregation of the people of Israel assembled at Shiloh, and set up the tent of meeting there; the land lay subdued before them. There remained among the people of Israel seven tribes whose inheritance (*naḥalah*) had not yet been apportioned (*ḥalequ*).[30] So Joshua said to the people of Israel, "How long will you be slack to go in and take possession (inherit; Hebrew *rešet*, Greek *klēronomēsai*) of the land, which the Lord, the God of your fathers, has given you? Provide three men from each tribe, and I will send them out that they may set out and go up and down the land, writing a description of it with a view to their inheritances (Hebrew *naḥalah*; Greek *dielein* [divide, distribute, apportion]), and then come to me. They[31] shall divide (Hebrew *tithallequ*; Greek *merisate* (from the same root as *meris* [portion]) it into seven portions (Hebrew *ḥalaqim*; Greek *meridas* [plural of *meris*]), Judah continuing in his territory on the south, and the house of Joseph in their territory on the north. And you shall describe (Hebrew "write"; Greek *merisate*) the land (earth) in seven divisions (Hebrew *ḥalaqim*; Greek *meridas*) and bring the description here to me; and I will cast *lots* (Greek *klēron* from the same root as *klēronomēsai* [inherit; receive through lots]) for you here before the Lord our God. The Levites have no portion (Hebrew *ḥeleq*; Greek *meris*) among you, for the priesthood of the Lord is their heritage (Hebrew *naḥalah*; Greek *meris*); and Gad and Reuben and half the tribe of Manasseh have received (Hebrew *laqeḥu*; Greek *elabosan* from the verb *lambanō*) their inheritance (*naḥalah*) beyond the Jordan eastward, which Moses the servant of the Lord gave them. So the men started on their way; and Joshua charged those who went to write the description of the land, saying, "Go up and down and write a description of the land, and come again to me; and I will cast *lots* (Hebrew *goral*; Greek *klēron*) for you here before the Lord in Shiloh." So the men went and passed up and down in the land and set down in a book a description of it by towns in seven divisions (Hebrew *ḥalaqim*; Greek *meridas*); then they came to Joshua in the camp at Shiloh,

---

[30] The LXX uses the verb *eklēronomēsan* to translate both the verb *ḥalequ* and its complement the noun *naḥalah*.

[31] "You" in both the MT and the LXX.

and Joshua cast *lots* (Hebrew *goral*; Greek *klēron*) for them in Shiloh before the Lord; and there Joshua apportioned (Hebrew *yeḥalleq*) the land to the people of Israel, to each his portion.[32] (18:1-10)

The terminology of both the MT and the LXX leaves no room for error in understanding the text's intention: Canaan is allocated through the medium of lots to the different tribes who are to live there, not as a single nation in the modern sense; the tribes are to enjoy it as shepherds enjoy their vast grazing area without hindrance *if they abide by the rules of the game.* Hindrance can come solely at the hand of the owner of that earth, who is the Lord himself, and his law is to be obeyed (1:1-11). The vast expanse of the territory (v.4), the scriptural Canaan promised to the "fathers" (Gen 6:4; 32:9), remains solely the Lord's possession to give conditionally to whom he pleases.

It remains for us to figure out what the "elusive" scriptural Canaan, where the Lord holds sway, is all about? On the basis of Joshua 1:4, one would expect that it is more a functional, rather than a tangible, reality. This is not as farfetched as it may seem given that "Canaanite' in scripture is often used as stand-in for a merchant who is keen on personal profit.[33] A good place to start our investigation is with the differentiation between the Cis-Jordan and Trans-Jordan areas of the tribal settlements. In Joshua this is clearly not so much a geographical matter as it is a matter of where the Lord's "heritage" lies. After the description of the heritage of the two and a half Trans-Jordan tribes (13:8-35), the text proceeds with the following statement: "And these are the inheritances which the people of Israel received in the

---

[32] The LXX omits the second half of the verse (and there Joshua apportioned [Hebrew *yeḥalleq*] the land to the people of Israel, to each his portion).

[33] See *C-Ezek* 196.

land of Canaan, which Eleazar the priest, and Joshua the son of Nun, and the heads of the fathers' houses of the tribes of the people of Israel distributed to them. Their inheritance was by lot, as the Lord had commanded Moses for the nine and one-half tribes." (14:1-2) Similarly, after the conclusion of the allotment process (21:43-45) we hear that "the Reubenites and the Gadites and the half-tribe of Manasseh returned home, parting from the people of Israel at Shiloh, which is *in the earth of Canaan,* to go *to the earth of Gilead, the earth of their possession* (Hebrew *'aḥuzzah*; Greek *kataskhesis*) which they *had possessed themselves* (Hebrew *no'ḥazu*; Greek *eklēronomēsan*) by command of the Lord through Moses." (22:9)[34] Thus, clearly the scriptural Canaan here is Cis-Jordan. The following verses tell us of a controversy between the Trans-Jordan tribes of Reuben, Gad, and half of Manasseh, on the one hand, and the rest of the tribes residing in Cis-Jordan, on the other hand, concerning the building of "an altar other than the altar of the Lord our God" (v.19). At one point in the debate Phinehas, the son of Eleazar the priest, and the accompanying ten tribal chiefs (22:13-14) address the Trans-Jordan brethren in these words: "But now, if *the earth of your possession* (Hebrew *'aḥuzzah*; Greek *kataskhesis*) is unclean, pass over *into the earth of the Lord's possession* (Hebrew *'aḥuzzah*; Greek *kataskhesis*) where the Lord's tabernacle stands, and *take for yourselves a possession* (Hebrew *he'aḥazzu*; Greek *kataklēronomēsate*) among us; only do not rebel against the Lord, or make us as rebels by building yourselves an altar other than the altar of the Lord our God." (v.19)[35] What is definitely striking in this case is that, although the allotments in Trans-

---

[34] My translation.
[35] My translation.

Jordan are "inheritances," they are not part of Canaan. How is one to "resolve" this apparent contradiction?

The unique scriptural instance of "the Lord's possession" (Hebrew 'ahuzzah; Greek kataskhesis) corroborates our earlier finding that, even after the settlement, the earth of the divine promise remains God's and solely his. And since he has no statue he is in no need of a temple of chiseled stones to house a statue of chiseled stones. His presence is reflected in his law, that is to say, his will for the people to obey, as is clear from the passage where we hear how the altar is defined:

> Then Joshua built an altar in Mount Ebal to the Lord, the God of Israel, as Moses the servant of the Lord had commanded the people of Israel, as it is written in the book of the law of Moses, "an altar of unhewn stones, upon which no man has lifted an iron tool"; and they offered on it burnt offerings to the Lord, and sacrificed peace offerings. And there, in the presence of the people of Israel, he wrote upon the stones a copy of the law of Moses, which he had written. And all Israel, sojourner as well as homeborn, with their elders and officers and their judges, stood on opposite sides of the ark before the Levitical priests who carried the ark of the covenant of the Lord, half of them in front of Mount Gerizim and half of them in front of Mount Ebal, as Moses the servant of the Lord had commanded at the first, that they should bless the people of Israel. And afterward he read all the words of the law, the blessing and the curse, according to all that is written in the book of the law. There was not a word of all that Moses commanded which Joshua did not read before all the assembly of Israel, and the women, and the little ones, and the sojourners who lived among them. (8:30-35)

The earth of the Lord's inheritance is any place where his will is observed. The copy altar that the Reubenites and the Gadites built and called "Witness; for it is a witness between us that the

Lord is God" (22:34) exemplifies this. Indeed, "witness" that is referred to thrice in this context (vv. 27, 28, 34), and for the first time in Joshua, will occur again four times in the last chapter of the book in a context dealing with the reading of the Law and its inscription for the ages to come, Joshua's last action:

> Then Joshua said to the people, "You are *witnesses* against yourselves that you have chosen the Lord, to serve him." And they said, "We are *witnesses*." He said, "Then put away the foreign gods which are among you, and incline your heart to the Lord, the God of Israel." And the people said to Joshua, "The Lord our God we will serve, and his voice we will obey." So Joshua made a covenant with the people that day, and made statutes and ordinances for them at Shechem. And Joshua wrote these words in the book of the law of God; and he took a great stone, and set it up there under the oak in the sanctuary of the Lord. And Joshua said to all the people, "Behold, this stone shall be a *witness* against us; for it has heard all the words of the Lord which he spoke to us; therefore it shall be a *witness* against you, lest you deal falsely with your God." So Joshua sent the people away, every man to his inheritance. After these things Joshua the son of Nun, the servant of the Lord, died, being a hundred and ten years old. (24:22-29)

Cis-Jordan alone, through the Kingdoms of Israel and Judah, will become functional in the subsequent story of the Prior Prophets. The scriptural Canaan is a symbolic stand-in for the area assigned by God, where the people and their wished for kings (1 Sam 8) will be tested in their obedience to his law (Judges 2:20-3:5), and where they will end up failing the test (2 Kg). Put otherwise, Canaan, the earth of God's heritage, will prove to be the area where the people earn the curse, rather than the blessing, of the Law (Lev 25; Deut 28; Joshua 8:34). Thus, Joshua functions as the prelude to the Prophets and leads to the full actualization of God's promises in the Latter Prophets where the "earth" (*'ereṣ*) of Canaan will be transformed through divine agency into a "ground" (*'adamah*) that will encompass every human being (*'adam*) under God's protection. As we shall see, such co-existence is already prefigured in Joshua itself. Furthermore, this scriptural story line will find its culmination in the third section of scripture, the Writings (*ketubim*), the literature that invites Israel to share with the "nations" the Law entrusted to it. Within the Writings one hears the Book of Job that tells the story of a Jew who was born and lived all his life outside Canaan yet, through his obedience to the Law, ended up reaping the blessings inscribed in it. In this sense, that book functions as the corrective to the disastrous story that plagues Canaan in the Prior Prophets and, by the same token, as an invitation to follow the lead of Ezekiel who heralded a Law-centered *Judaism* around the synagogues spread throughout God's earth of Genesis 1 against a doomed *Judah* that insisted on finding its hope in the stones its hands had built (Jer 7).[36] After the promulgation of the Law in the Mosaic Five Books, Joshua stands as the opening chapter in the scriptural hyperbolic story whose moral sounds thus: divine blessing promised in the Law comes by living on the only earth we have, while recognizing that it is God's "heritage" and not our "property." Put in scriptural terms it is the people themselves who are God's property insofar as they obey him: "Now therefore, if you will obey my voice and keep my covenant, you shall be my own possession among all peoples; for all the earth is mine." (Ex 19:5) It is precisely this teaching that Paul will eventually make binding on his Gentiles: "You are not your own; you were bought with a price." (1 Cor 6:19b-20a)

---

[36] *C-Ezek* 270-6.

2

The Command to Joshua

Be Strong and of Good Courage

Beginning with Joshua's first action, which is a command (Josh 1:10), the book relates the unfolding of the tribes' entrance into Canaan during Joshua's lifetime, and their settlement in it among its original residents. God works out his salvation for the people through the special help he offers to Joshua, Moses' minister, on the condition that he stick closely to the divine law:

"Be strong and of good courage (*ḥazaq we'emeṣ*); for you shall cause this people to inherit (*tanḥil*) the land which I swore to their fathers to give them. Only (*raq*) be strong and very courageous (*ḥazaq we'emeṣ*), being careful (Hebrew *lišmor* [from *šamar*]; Greek *phylassesthai*; in order to keep) to do (Hebrew *la'aśot* [from *'aśah*]; Greek *poiein*) according to all the law which Moses my servant commanded you; turn not from it to the right hand or to the left, that you may have good success (Hebrew *taśkil*; Greek *synēs*; be wise, understanding) wherever you go (*telek*; walk). This book of the law shall not depart out of your mouth, but you shall meditate (*hagetah*) on it day and night, that you may be careful (*tišmor* [from *šamar*]; in order to keep) to do (Hebrew *la'aśot* [from *'aśah*]; Greek *poiein*) according to all that is written in it; for then you shall make your way prosperous (*taṣliaḥ*), and then you shall have good success (Hebrew *taśkil*; Greek *synēseis*; be wise, understanding). Have I not commanded you? Be strong and of good courage (*ḥazaq we'emeṣ*); be not frightened (*ta'aroṣ*), neither be dismayed (*teḥat*); for the Lord your God is with you wherever you go." Then Joshua commanded the officers of the people, "Pass through the camp, and command the people, 'Prepare your provisions; for within three days you are to pass over this Jordan, to go in to take possession of the land which the Lord your God gives you to possess.'" (vv.6-11)

When hearing this passage in English, especially with the terminology "be strong" and "be courageous," combined with "prosperous" and "success," and ending with "possession," one gets the distinct impression that it is all about a military campaign. Most notable translations, such as KJV, JB, and RSV, and most hearers, view the Book of Joshua as such. However, the book is not so much about conquest as it is about the allocation of a heritage.

Of paramount importance is that these verses repeat what was heard a few chapters earlier on Moses' lips in his address to Joshua as well as to "all Israel":

So Moses continued to speak these words to all Israel. And he said to them, "I am a hundred and twenty years old this day; I am no longer able to go out and come in. The Lord has said to me, 'You shall not go over this Jordan.' The Lord your God himself will go over before you; he will destroy these nations before you and *you shall become the inheritor instead of them* (Hebrew *wiristam*; Greek *kataklēronomēseis avtous*); and Joshua will go over at your head, as the Lord has spoken. And the Lord will do to them as he did to Sihon and Og, the kings of the Amorites, and to their land, when he destroyed them. And the Lord will give them over to you, and you shall do to them according to all the commandment which I have commanded you. Be strong and of good courage (*ḥizqu we'imṣu*), do not fear (*tire'u*) or be in dread (*ta'arṣu*) of them: for it is the Lord your God who goes with you; he will not fail you or forsake you." Then Moses summoned Joshua, and said to him in the sight of all Israel, "Be strong and of good courage (*ḥazaq we'emeṣ*); for you shall go with this people into the land which the

Lord has sworn to their fathers to give them; and you shall put
them in possession (Hebrew *tanḥilennah*; cause them to inherit;
Greek *kataklēronomēseis*) of it. It is the Lord who goes before you;
he will be with you, he will not fail you or forsake you; do not fear
(*tira'*) or be dismayed (*teḥat*)." And Moses *wrote this law*, and gave
it to the priests the sons of Levi, who carried the ark of the
covenant of the Lord, and to all the elders of Israel ... Moses
commanded the Levites who carried the ark of the covenant of the
Lord, "Take this book of the law, and put it by the side of the ark
of the covenant of the Lord your God, that it may be there for a
witness against you." (Deut 31:1-9, 25-26)

It is evident then that the strength and the courage required of
Joshua (Josh 1:6, 7, 9) have nothing to do with personal
prowess. Rather they have to do with Joshua's zeal in abiding by
the Law's divine commandments. This idea pervades the Book of
Deuteronomy right from the start: "The Lord was angry with me
[Moses] also on your account, and said, 'You also shall not go in
there; Joshua the son of Nun, who stands before you, he shall
enter; encourage (*ḥazzeq*) him, for he shall cause Israel to inherit
it (Hebrew *yanḥilennah*; Greek *kataklēronomēsei*).'" (1:37-38) A
cursive hearing of Deuteronomy will reveal that its terminology
and spirit are echoed in Joshua 1:6-11:

But charge (*ṣaw*; command) and Joshua, and encourage and
strengthen him (*weḥazzeqehu we'mmeṣehu*); for he shall go over at
the head of this people, and he shall put them in possession
(*yanḥil*) of the land which you shall see. (Deut 3:28)

Hear therefore, O Israel, and be careful (*šamarta*; keep) to do
them (*la'aśot*); that it may go well with you, and that you may
multiply greatly, as the Lord, the God of your fathers, has
promised you, in a land flowing with milk and honey. (6:3)

And because (*'eqeb*; as a result of) you hearken to these ordinances, and keep (*šemartem*) and do them (*'aśitem*), the Lord your God will keep (*šamar*) with you the covenant and the steadfast love which he swore to your fathers to keep.[1] (7:12)

All the commandment which I command you this day you shall be careful (*tišmerun*; keep) to do (*la'aśot*), that you may live and multiply, and go in and possess (*yerištem*; inherit) the land which the Lord swore to give to your fathers. (8:1)

You shall therefore keep (*šemartem*) all the commandment which I command you this day, that (*lema'an*; in order to) you may be strong (*tehezqu*), and go in and take possession (*yerištem*; inherit) of the land which you are going over to possess (*lerištah*; to inherit).[2] (11:8)

For if you will *be careful to do* (*šamor tišmerun*; keep indeed, fully) all this commandment which I command you to do, loving the Lord your God, walking in all his ways,[3] and cleaving to him, then the Lord will drive out (*horiš*; make you inheritors instead of) all these nations before you, and you will dispossess (*yerištem*; inherit) nations greater and mightier than yourselves. (11:22-23)

For you are to pass over the Jordan to go in to take possession of (*larešet*; to inherit) the land which the Lord your God gives you; and when you possess (*yerištem*; inherit) it and live in it, you shall be careful (*šemartem*; keep) to do (*la'aśot*) all the statutes and the ordinances which I set before you this day. These are the statutes and ordinances which you shall be careful (*tišmerun*; keep) to do

---

[1] Notice the wordplay reflecting God's "keeping" his covenant as contingent on the people's "keeping" his commandments.

[2] Notice how here the inheritance is the direct outcome of obedience to the commandments, without the medium of military force.

[3] This is the same terminology as found in Josh 1:7: "Only be strong and very courageous, being careful to do according to all the law which Moses my servant commanded you; turn not from it to the right hand or to the left, that you may have good success wherever you go."

(*la'aśot*) in the land which the Lord, the God of your fathers, has given you to possess (*leriśtah*; to inherit), all the days that you live upon the earth.[4] (11:31-12:1)

This day the Lord your God commands you to do these statutes and ordinances; you shall therefore be careful (*šamarta*; keep) to do (*'aśita*) them with all your heart and with all your soul.[5] (26:16)

If you are not careful (*tiśamor*; keep) to do (*la'aśot*) all the words of *this law which are written in this book*, that you may fear this glorious and awful name, the Lord your God. (28:58)

"Be strong and of good courage (*ḥazaq we'emeṣ*)" (Josh 1:6, 7, 9) is encountered in Deuteronomy in conjunction with either the Law and its statutes, or the inheritance of Canaan, or with both. The conjunction "only" (*raq*; Josh 1:7) is also often found in Deuteronomy in relation to keeping the Law's injunctions, and regarding the inheritance as well:

And what great nation is there, that has statutes and ordinances so righteous as all this law which I set before you this day? *Only* (*raq*) take heed, and keep your soul diligently, lest you forget the things which your eyes have seen, and lest they depart from your heart all the days of your life; make them known to your children and your children's children. (4:8-9)

Take heed that you do not offer your burnt offerings at every place that you see; but at the place which the Lord will choose in one of your tribes, there you shall offer your burnt offerings, and there you shall do all that I am commanding you. *However* (*raq*), you may slaughter and eat flesh within any of your towns, as much as you desire, according to the blessing of the Lord your God which

---

[4] See previous footnote. It is obvious that the phrase "all the days that you live upon the earth" is to be taken with "to do" and not "to inherit."

[5] See also 28:1, 13, 15.

he has given you; the unclean and the clean may eat of it, as of the gazelle and as of the hart. *Only (raq)* you shall not eat the blood; you shall pour it out upon the earth like water.[6] (12:13-16)

But there will be no poor among you (for the Lord will bless you in the land which the Lord your God gives you for an inheritance (*naḥalah*) to possess (*leriŝtah*; to inherit), if *only (raq)* you will obey the voice of the Lord your God, being careful to do all this commandment which I command you this day. (15:4-5)

The phrase "turn to the right hand or to the left" (Josh 1:7) is found throughout Deuteronomy:

You shall be careful to do therefore as the Lord your God has commanded you; you shall not turn aside to the right hand or to the left. (5:32)

Then you shall do according to what they declare to you from that place which the Lord will choose; and you shall be careful to do according to all that they direct you; according to the instructions which they give you, and according to the decision which they pronounce to you, you shall do; you shall not turn aside from the verdict which they declare to you, either to the right hand or to the left. (17:10-11)

And when he sits on the throne of his kingdom, he shall write for himself in a book a copy of this law, from that which is in the charge of the Levitical priests; and it shall be with him, and he shall read in it all the days of his life, that he may learn to fear the Lord his God, by keeping all the words of this law and these statutes, and doing them; that his heart may not be lifted up above his brethren, and that he may not turn aside from the commandment, either to the right hand or to the left; so that he

---

[6] See also 12:23, 26; 15:22-23.

may continue long in his kingdom, he and his children, in Israel. (17:18-20)

And the Lord will make you the head, and not the tail; and you shall tend upward only, and not downward; if you obey the commandments of the Lord your God, which I command you this day, being careful to do them, and if you do not turn aside from any of the words which I command you this day, to the right hand or to the left, to go after other gods to serve them. (28:13-14)

Finally, the last "be strong and of good courage (*ḥazaq we'emeṣ*)" which introduces "be not frightened (*ta'aroṣ*), neither be dismayed (*teḥat*); for the Lord your God is with you wherever you go" (Joshua 1: 9) is a shortened version of what one just heard in Deuteronomy:

"Be strong and of good courage (*ḥizqu we'imṣu*),[7] do not fear or be in dread (*ta'arṣu*)[8] of them: for it is the Lord your God who goes with you; he will not fail you or forsake you." Then Moses summoned Joshua, and said to him in the sight of all Israel, "Be strong and of good courage (*ḥazaq we'emeṣ*); for you shall go with this people into the land which the Lord has sworn to their fathers to give them; and you shall put them in possession of (*tanḥilennah*; make [them] inherit) it. It is the Lord who goes before you; he will be with you, he will not fail you or forsake you; do not fear or be dismayed (*teḥat*)." (31:6-8)

At the beginning of Deuteronomy, these two verbs appeared in the passage dealing with the people's incredulity at Kadeshbarnea (1:19-33): "Behold, the Lord your God has set the land before you; go up, take possession (*reš*; inherit), as the Lord, the God of

---

[7] The plural form of *ḥazaq we'emeṣ*.

[8] The plural form of *ta'aroṣ*.

your fathers, has told you; do not fear or be dismayed (*tehat*) ... Then I said to you, 'Do not be in dread (*ta'arṣun*) or afraid of them.'" (vv.21, 29)[9]

Thus the reliance of Joshua 1:6-11 on Deuteronomy is firmly established. However, the meaning and intention of the original Hebrew has been totally obfuscated by RSV, and JB for that matter, since these translations exude success of a military campaign.[10] The Hebrew of v.7b is "turn not from it to the right hand or to the left, that *taskil* wherever (in all that) *telek*." *taskil* means "you be prudent, you have insight, you have understanding, you have wisdom" as corroborated by its LXX rendering as *synēs* from the verb *syniēmi* whose meaning is "understand, comprehend, have insight into." On the other hand, *telek* is from the verb *halak* meaning "walk." This verb is used throughout scripture to refer to walking the "way" of the Law, and thus behaving according to its commandments. Once more, this is corroborated in the LXX that has *prassēs*, the unequivocal meaning of which is "you practice, you do, you behave." Consequently, whatever "success" Joshua is supposed to have or reap is not connected to military victories, but rather to his behaving according to the Law, the utterance of which is not to depart from his mouth day and night. Military victories are explicitly the domain and duty of "the commander of the Lord's army" (5:13-15). This is further confirmed by what one hears in 1:8: "that you may be careful (*tišmor* [from *šamar*]; in order to keep) to do (Hebrew *la'aśot* [from *'aśah*]; Greek *poiein*) according

---

[9] See also Deut 7:21 (You shall not be in dread [*ta'aroṣ*] of them; for the Lord your God is in the midst of you, a great and terrible God) and 20:3 (Hear, O Israel, you draw near this day to battle against your enemies: let not your heart faint; do not fear, or tremble, or be in dread [*ta'arṣu*] of them).

[10] Notice even RSV's preposterous "good success" as though there could be "bad success"!

to all that is written in it,"[11] and by what we hear in Deuteronomy:

> Behold, I have taught you statutes and ordinances, as the Lord my God commanded me, that you should do them in the land which you are entering to take possession of it (*leristah*; to inherit it). Keep them and do them; for that will be your *wisdom* (*hokmah*; Greek *sophia*) and your *understanding* (*binah*; Greek *synesis* [from the same root as *synēs* in Joshua]) in the sight of the peoples, who, when they hear all these statutes, will say, "Surely this great nation is a wise (*hakam*; Greek *sophos*) and understanding (*nabon*; Greek *epistēmōn*) people." (4:5-6)

> Therefore be careful to do the words of this covenant, that you may prosper (Hebrew *taskilu*; Greek *synēte*; be wise, understanding)[12] in all that you do. (29:9)

> If you obey the commandments of the Lord your God which I command you this day, by loving the Lord your God, by walking (*laleket* [from the verb *halak* found in Joshua]) in his ways *bidrakaw*) and by keeping his commandments and his statutes and his ordinances, then you shall live and multiply, and the Lord

---

[11]The Greek *poiein* is the twin verb of *prassein* in scripture as we hear in the classic Pauline text dealing with behavior according to the Law's injunctions: "Though they know God's decree that those who do (*prassontes*) such things deserve to die, they not only do (*poiousin*) them but approve those who practice (*prassousin*) them. Therefore you have no excuse, O man, whoever you are, when you judge another; for in passing judgment upon him you condemn yourself, because you, the judge, are doing (*prasseis*) the very same things. We know that the judgment of God rightly falls upon those who do (*prassontas*) such things. Do you suppose, O man, that when you judge those who do (*prassontas*) such things and yet do (*poiōn*) them yourself, you will escape the judgment of God?" (Rom 1:32-2:3)

[12] In both cases, Hebrew and Greek, these verbs are the plural of what we hear in Josh 1:7.

your God will bless you in the land which you are entering to take
possession of it (*leristah*; to inherit it). (30:16)

The last two quotations confirm that "walking" in scripture is
tantamount to "behaving." In 30:16, "walking on the way (of
God)" is tantamount to "keeping his commandments," whereas
"all that you do" in 29:9 corresponds to "wherever you walk"
("make your way" in RSV) in Joshua 1:8. Accordingly, "the way"
referred to in the latter verse does not refer to Joshua's alleged
"military campaign," but rather to his behaving according to the
Law's commandments. Doing such will ensure *tasliah*, which
RSV mistranslates as "prosperity." The original Hebrew has the
connotation of "putting something in order," "bringing
something to the situation in which it ought to be," and,
consequently, "finding the right way to do so." Only in this
sense can one find success in one's endeavor.[13] Again this finds
confirmation in Deuteronomy:

> The Lord will smite you with madness and blindness and
> confusion of mind (*lebab*; heart); and you shall grope at noonday,
> as the blind grope in darkness, and you shall not prosper in
> (*tasliah*; correct, put in order) your ways (*derakeka*); and you shall
> be only oppressed and robbed continually, and there shall be no
> one to help you. (28:28-29)

As is usual in many literary triads, the central element is the
most important; the other two are used for underscoring. This is
clearly the case in v.29a as blindness is the subject matter: "and
you shall grope at noonday, as the blind grope in darkness." By
the same token, the latter part of the comment (and you shall
not prosper in [*tasliah*] your ways [*derakeka*]) is the result of the
preceding. By translating "and you shall not prosper in your

---

[13] Those who know Arabic will recall the causative *'aslaha*.

ways" instead of "and you shall not correct (bring into order—
which is the opposite of grope) your ways," RSV and KJV seem
to read this in conjunction with "and you shall be only oppressed
and robbed continually, and there shall be no one to help you."
Such a translation is questionable. JB opts to start another
paragraph with this statement, thus making it an introduction to
the following verses 30-35 which give a series of detailed
examples that describe being "oppressed and robbed" (KJV
spoiled). However, when one takes "and you shall not correct
(bring into order—which is the opposite of grope) your ways" as
counterpart to "and you shall grope at noonday, as the blind
grope in darkness," then the description of blindness makes full
sense. Still, the author's subtlety is evident in his addition of
"mind (*lebab*; heart)" to qualify "confusion." "Heart" in scripture
is the human being's mental center with which one thinks,
deliberates, and decides, as well as feels; that is why it takes
central stage in the Law whenever it deals with one's attitude
toward God. What is intended in this passage is that the
consequence of blindness to the Law's dictates is not being able
to find the right "way." This conclusion imposes itself in that
Deuteronomy 28:28-29 are part of the second section of the
chapter (vv.15-68) that deals with the curses one incurs if one
does not abide by the divine law: "But if you will not obey the
voice of the Lord your God or be careful to do all his
commandments (*miṣwot*, plural of *miṣwah*) and his statutes
which I command (*ṣiwweh*) you this day, then all these curses
shall come upon you and overtake you." (v.15) The first and
shorter section of the chapter (vv.1-14) deals with the blessings
resulting from one's obedience to that same Law: "And if you
obey the voice of the Lord your God, being careful to do all his
commandments (*miṣwot*, plural of *miṣwah*) which I command
(*ṣiwweh*) you this day, the Lord your God will set you high above

all the nations of the earth. And all these blessings shall come upon you and overtake you, if you obey the voice of the Lord your God." (vv.1-2) Going back to Joshua, one finds further corroboration in that 1:6-11 ends with the thrice repeated verb *ṣiwweh* (command) that is from the same root as the noun *miṣwah* (commandment): God commands Joshua (v.9) who, in turn, commands the officers of the people (v.10) requiring them to command the people (v.11).

This is precisely how the LXX understood the matter. In Deuteronomy 28:29 it translates *taṣliaḥ derakeka* into *evodōsei tas hodous sou*, which is "he [the blind person] will straighten (find the right direction for, bring to the right conclusion) his paths (ways)." What is striking, though, is that the same LXX gives a clarifying translation of the original Joshua 1:8b. While the Hebrew reads "[in order] that you keep to do (hold unto doing) according to all that is written in it; for then you shall straighten your ways, and then you shall have understanding,"[14] the LXX has "[in order] that you understand (*synēs*) [in order] to do according to all that is written in it, then *you shall be straightened on the correct path* (*evodōthēsē*), and you shall straighten (*evodōseis*) your ways (*tas hodous sou*), then you shall have understanding (*synēseis*)." It creates an *inclusio* ABB'A' where "walking on the straight path" is flanked by "understanding." Opting for "understanding" instead of the original "keeping" before "to do" makes sense in view of the LXX's rendering of the Hebrew *hagetah* into *meletēseis* (you shall meditate [think, research])—thinking requires understanding. However, there is more to this than strikes the ear. When it comes to commandments or statutes, the Hebrew *šamar* (keep) does not

---

[14] *lema'an tišmor la'aśot kekol hakkatub bo ki-'az taṣliaḥ et-derakeka we'az taśkil.*

mean "keep in store, hold physically to," or even "keep them *in mind*," but rather *meaning wise* "hold to them," "be aware of them *and their intention*" in order to act upon their injunctions." So the LXX was preparing for the second *synēseis* (you shall have understanding, you shall acquire wisdom), which is the technical meaning of the Hebrew *taśkil.* Thus it remains for us to explain why the LXX splits the original one *taṣliaḥ* into two parts *evodōthēsē* (you shall be straightened on the correct path) and *evodōseis tas hodous sou* (you shall straighten your ways) here, yet kept only the latter in Deuteronomy. The addition actually boils down to the passive tense *evodōthēsē* since *taṣliaḥ* is an active tense verb. Its function is to draw the hearer's attention to the fact that "successes" on one's "paths" are the result of these being straightened by one's understanding and *doing* the Law's commandments *in the earth of Canaan.* It in no way refers to military achievements.

Before leaving this passage one last note concerning the original Hebrew is in order since it will both wrap up our discussion and confirm our findings. What is commonly translated as "meditate," following the Greek *meletēseis*, is the Hebrew *hagita* from the verb *hagah* that has the technical meaning of "spell" the consonants of a word[15] and thus "mutter," "read in an undertone," "talk to oneself." Only in this last sense one can extrapolate "ponder" or "meditate." Thus the meaning of *hagah* is "recite from memory."[16] One would have to

---

[15] Those who know Arabic will recognize the corresponding *tahajja.* In Arabic the letter of the alphabet corresponding to the Hebrew *g* is pronounced *j*; Egyptians still pronounce it *g*.

[16] It is that same verb that is encountered in Ps 1:2: "Blessed is the man who *walks* not in the counsel of the wicked, nor stands on the way of sinners, nor sits in the seat of scoffers; but his delight is in the law of the Lord, and on his law he meditates (*yehgeh*; mutters, recites) day and night." (vv. 1-2) It is obviously such muttering that reminds

spend much time, "day and night" (Josh 1:8), reciting the Law again and again to master its content by heart. It is only when one does so that there will be no need to "see" the book in order to "read it" and that "this book of the law shall not depart out of your mouth"—a mouth which will be reciting the book, not reading it. Joshua would not have been able to get to that point if he had to spend time planning and executing military campaigns. That is why the latter duty is relegated to "the commander of the Lord's army" (5:13-15).

---

the man of the content of the Law and invites him to follow its injunctions; *only in so doing*, he is preserved from "walking" (behaving) according to the counsel of the wicked and is "blessed." That is to say, the right behavior is the *result and consequence* of remembering the content of the Law.

3

The Trans-Jordan Tribes

The Proprietor of the Heritage

By bracketing his overarching story with reference to the two and a half tribes whose allotments did not fall within Canaan (Josh 1:12-18 and ch.22), the author undoubtedly wanted to underscore his introductory message (1:1-11): the ground where Israel is about to dwell is a heritage whose proprietor is God; he will forever remain its Lord and, over the generations, will assign it to whomever he wills. It is as though the author was reminding the hearers that, although the abode of those two and a half tribes was outside Canaan, their dwelling ground was nonetheless still a heritage from the Lord. As will be stressed in chapter 22, the corollary is that these tribes are no less bound to the divine law than those dwelling in Canaan. Thus the beginning of Joshua is looking ahead toward the Latter Prophets and, beyond them, to the Writings, whose teaching is that the protective "fence" around God's congregation is not the boundary of its allotment, but rather the observance of the Law wherever one happens to be (see especially the Book of Job).

This reading is supported by the author's choice for the Transjordan tribes. Reuben was Jacob's first born (Gen 29:32), and it would have been both legal and fitting that his heritage fall within Canaan, yet it did not. Gad was another Reuben, so to speak. He came as the first in a new group of children to Leah and was given the name "good fortune," and yet his descendants did not have the good fortune to settle in Canaan:

> When Leah saw that she had ceased bearing children, she took her
> maid Zilpah and gave her to Jacob as a wife. Then Leah's maid

Zilpah bore Jacob a son. And Leah said, "Good fortune!" (*gad*) so she called his name Gad. (30:9-11)

Finally, Manasseh was the first born of Joseph (41:51). Without Joseph's intervention, Israel would have perished in Egypt. So important is Joseph that his bones were carried out of Egypt all the way to Canaan and finally buried at Shechem (Josh 24:32). Thus, to relegate an inheritance outside Canaan to Reuben, Gad, and half of the tribe of Manasseh is strange, to say the least, unless one considers it intentional on the part of the author: a reminder that no one is *entitled* to the inheritance, which always remains a prerogative of the "father" (Gal 4:1-2). Such cannot be but a prelude to what will be spelled out in chapter 23 where we shall hear that Israel's fate in Canaan is no better than that of the nations before it:

And now I am about to go the way of all the earth, and you know in your hearts and souls, all of you, that not one thing has failed of all the good things which the Lord your God promised concerning you; all have come to pass for you, not one of them has failed. But just as all the good things which the Lord your God promised concerning you have been fulfilled for you, so the Lord will bring upon you all the evil things, until he have destroyed (*hašmid*) you from off this good land which the Lord your God has given you, if you transgress the covenant of the Lord your God, which he commanded you, and go and serve other gods and bow down to them. Then the anger of the Lord will be kindled against you, and you shall perish quickly from off the good land which he has given to you. (23:14-16)

Israel has been made aware, in no uncertain terms, of God's equality in dealing with all people:

Do not say in your heart, after the Lord your God has thrust them out before you, "It is because of my righteousness that the Lord has brought me in to possess this land"; whereas it is *because of the wickedness of these nations* that the Lord is driving them out before you. Not because of your righteousness or the uprightness of your heart are you going in to possess (to inherit) their land; but *because of the wickedness of these nations* the Lord your God is driving them out from before you, and that he may confirm the word which the Lord swore to your fathers, to Abraham, to Isaac, and to Jacob. Know therefore, that the Lord your God is not giving you this good land to possess (to inherit) because of your righteousness; for you are a stubborn people. (Deut 9:4-6)

If you are not careful to do all the words of this law which are written in this book, that you may fear this glorious and awful name, the Lord your God, then the Lord will bring on you and your offspring extraordinary afflictions, afflictions severe and lasting, and sicknesses grievous and lasting … And as the Lord took delight in doing you good and multiplying you, so the Lord will take delight in bringing ruin upon you and destroying (*hašmid*) you; and you shall be plucked off the land which you are entering to take possession of (to inherit) it. And the Lord will scatter you among all peoples, from one end of the earth to the other; and there you shall serve other gods, of wood and stone, which neither you nor your fathers have known. And *among these nations* you shall find no ease, and there shall be no rest for the sole of your foot; but the Lord will give you there a trembling heart, and failing eyes, and a languishing soul; your life shall hang in doubt before you; night and day you shall be in dread, and have no assurance of your life. (28:58-59, 63-66)

Still, Joshua's injunction includes another important reminder, which is that God's congregation, the scriptural Israel, is one and its fate is all inclusive, that is, the Lord establishes all, preserves all, punishes all, and at the end restores the remnant into a new encompassing *one* congregation:

What is in your mind shall never happen—the thought, "Let us be
like the nations, like the tribes of the countries, and worship wood
and stone." As I live, says the Lord God, surely with a mighty
hand and an outstretched arm, and with wrath poured out, I will
be king over you. I will bring you out from the peoples and gather
you out of the countries where you are scattered, with a mighty
hand and an outstretched arm, and with wrath poured out; and I
will bring you into the wilderness of the peoples, and there I will
enter into judgment with you face to face. As I entered into
judgment with your fathers in the wilderness of the land of Egypt,
so I will enter into judgment with you, says the Lord God. I will
make you pass under the rod, and I will let you go in by number. *I
will purge out the rebels from among you, and those who transgress
against me; I will bring them out of the land where they sojourn, but
they shall not enter the land of Israel.* Then you will know that I am
the Lord. As for you, O house of Israel, thus says the Lord God:
Go serve every one of you his idols, now and hereafter, if you will
not listen to me; but my holy name you shall no more profane
with your gifts and your idols. For on my holy mountain, the
mountain height of Israel, says the Lord God, *there all the house of
Israel, all of them, shall serve me in the land*; there I will accept
them, and there I will require your contributions and the choicest
of your gifts, with all your sacred offerings. (Ezek 20:32-40)

To insure this oneness of the fate, the adult men of the
Transjordan tribes may not rest within their allotted heritage
until their brethren of the other nine and a half tribes have rested
in theirs in Canaan (Josh 1:13-15). The intransigence of that
condition is evident in the response of the Reubenites, the
Gadites, and the half-tribe of Manasseh (vv.16-18). Those tribes
endorse Joshua's mission with the same words used by God
himself: "Only be strong and of good courage." (v.18b; see v.7a).
Anyone who does not submit to the utterances of Joshua's
mouth (v.18a) while he is mumbling the words of the Law (v.8)
will be considered a "rebel" and put to death.

In retrospect, one realizes how the author's choice of the Transjordan tribes was done in view of the subsequent rendering of the story consigned in the Prophets. The fate of the one congregation was determined by the obedience or disobedience of the monarchs of the two kingdoms that covered the territory of Canaan: the Kingdom of Judah, whose capital was Jerusalem, and that of Israel, whose capital was Samaria (often addressed by the prophets as Joseph or Ephraim). Reuben and Gad are closely linked to Judah in that all three are of the progeny of Jacob through Leah (Gen 29:31-30:11). Manasseh and Ephraim are the sons of Joseph (41:50-52) who is of the progeny of Rachel (30:22-24), Jacob's other wife.

4

Rahab

Although chapter 2 is introduced thrice as being about the spying on the earth of Canaan (vv.1, 2, 3) one does not learn anything about such activity. It is the harlot Rahab who steals the spotlight; the entire chapter functions as an explanation as to why she and her entire kindred are spared (ch.6). She is introduced early in the story (2:1b), and the hearers are left curious to learn more about her. Their curiosity will be satisfied since the chapter will prove to be about the oath taken by the spies to protect Rahab and her family (vv.12, 17, 20). A keen ear will not miss the connection with the previous reference to oath: in 1:6 it is the Lord who swears to the fathers that their children will inherit Canaan, here in 2:12 the spies are asked to swear by that same Lord that Rahab and her kindred will fully share in that inheritance:

> And they burned the city with fire, and all within it; only the silver and gold, and the vessels of bronze and of iron, they put into the treasury of the house of the Lord. But Rahab the harlot, and her father's household, and all who belonged to her, Joshua saved alive; and *she dwelt in (the midst of; beqereb) Israel to this day*, because she hid the messengers whom Joshua sent to spy out Jericho. (6:24-25)

In other words, the story of Rahab the "harlot" (2:1; 6:17, 22, 25) is a lesson for Israel, which committed harlotry in the wilderness, not to do the same in Canaan lest they themselves end up destroyed on the earth of promise (22:14-16). And this is what scripture is all about: not so much to point the finger at the nations that are, by definition, "sinners" (Gal 2:15), but rather to invite the members of God's congregation not to fall away from their commitment to him by following "foreign gods," which is scriptural "harlotry." [1]

This reading finds unequivocal corroboration in the use of two nouns Shittim and Rahab which occur in Joshua 2:1 and control the entire story of that chapter. Although Rahab is obviously the main character of the story, the double mention of Shittim at the start (2:1) and at the end (3:1)—which are the only two instances of that noun in the Prior Prophets—gives the hearer the distinct impression that the story is an interlude while the people was sojourning at Shittim.[2] The importance of this for our story concerning Rahab the "harlot" (Hebrew *zonah*; Greek *pornē*) and the entrance into Canaan is corroborated in how Shittim functions in its previous two occurrences:

> While Israel dwelt in Shittim the people began to play the harlot with the daughters of Moab. These invited the people to the sacrifices of their gods, and the people ate, and bowed down to their gods. So Israel yoked himself to Baal of Peor. And the anger of the Lord was kindled against Israel; and the Lord said to Moses, "Take all the chiefs of the people, and hang them in the sun before

---

[1] Paul wrote in 1 Corinthians: "I wrote to you in my letter not to associate with immoral men (*pornois*: fornicators); not at all meaning the immoral (*pornois*: fornicators) of this world, or the greedy and robbers, or *idolaters*, since then you would need to go out of the world. But rather I wrote to you not to associate with any one who bears the name of brother if he is *guilty of immorality* (*pornos*; fornicator, harlot) or greed, or is an *idolater*, reviler, drunkard, or robber— not even to eat with such a one. *For what have I to do with judging outsiders? Is it not those inside the church whom you are to judge? God judges those outside. 'Drive out the wicked person from among you.'*" (5:9-13) See also Col 3:5: "Put to death therefore what is earthly in you: fornication (*porneian*; harlotry), impurity, passion, evil desire, and covetousness, which is idolatry."

[2] A similar kind of interlude is found in the story of Abraham going down to Egypt (Gen 12:10-20) that took place while his tent was pitched at Bethel (12:8; 13:3).

the Lord, that the fierce anger of the Lord may turn away from Israel." And Moses said to the judges of Israel, "Every one of you slay his men who have yoked themselves to Baal of Peor." (Num 25:1-5)

And they [the children of Israel;[3] 33:5] set out from the mountains of Abarim, and encamped in the plains of Moab by the Jordan at Jericho; they encamped by the Jordan from Bethjeshimoth[4] as far as Abel-shittim[5] in the plains of Moab. And the Lord said to Moses in the plains of Moab by the Jordan at Jericho, "Say to the people of Israel, When you pass over the Jordan into the land of Canaan, then you shall drive out (inherit instead of) all the inhabitants of the land from before you, and destroy all their figured stones, and destroy all their molten images, and demolish all their high places; and you shall take possession of (inherit) the land and settle in it, for I have given the land to you to possess it (inherit). You shall inherit the land by lot according to your families; to a large tribe you shall give a large inheritance, and to a small tribe you shall give a small inheritance; wherever the lot falls to any man, that shall be his; according to the tribes of your fathers you shall inherit. But if you do not drive out (inherit instead of) the inhabitants of the land from before you, then those of them whom you let remain shall be as pricks in your eyes and thorns in your sides, and they shall trouble you in the land where you dwell. And I will do to you as I thought to do to them." (33:48-56)

So the mention of Shittim in Joshua is a subtle reminder to the hearers that it is, in fact, Israel that is disobedient to God, whereas Rahab confesses that "the Lord your God is he who is God in heaven above and on earth beneath" (2:11) and submits to his will.

---

[3] RSV has "the people of Israel."
[4] The original Hebrew means "the house of devastations."
[5] The original Hebrew means "the brook of Shittim."

A keen ear will detect yet another facet of the name Shittim, which is functional in the story of the entrance into Canaan. The Hebrew *šiṭṭim* is the plural of *šiṭṭah*, the acacia tree. Aside from Isaiah 41:19 where the singular is used (I will put in the wilderness the cedar, the acacia [*šiṭṭah*], the myrtle, and the olive; I will set in the desert the cypress, the plane and the pine together), all the other occurrences are in the plural form and are found exclusively in Exodus with the exception of Deuteronomy 10:3. In all those instances *šiṭṭim* refers to the acacia wood from which the ark of the covenant is made, as are the different components of the tabernacle. It is precisely the ark of the covenant which will lead the procession into Canaan (Josh 3; 4; 6) and around which every word of the Law will be read "before all the assembly of Israel, and the women, and the little ones, and the sojourners who lived among them" (8:35).

It is against this background that Rahab is given as the example to be followed by Israel should the latter decide to remain in Canaan. The Hebrew name *raḥab*, found only in Joshua (2:1; 3:6:17, 23, 25) in the entire Old Testament, is from a root, *rḥb*, meaning "width, breadth, open area;" "wide, large."[6] Earlier in Genesis this root was encountered in passages related to either the earth of sojourn of the Patriarchs or to the rule of hospitality. The only exception is its use in describing the breadth of Noah's ark (Gen 6:15). An extensive study of the root *rḥb* is in order

---

[6] The mythical sea monster Rahab is from a different root, the middle letter *h* being a different consonant than the one found in the harlot's name and in the terms connected with "width." The Hebrew language has two different consonants ה (sounding as our "h" as in "home;" this is the second letter of the noun Rahab [the sea monster]) and ח (found in the name Rachel as well as [the harlot] Rahab, and thus often transliterated as "ch"). The official transliteration of ה is *h* and that of ח is *ḥ*. The root *rhb* has the connotation of "terror."

since it is precisely the misunderstanding of this root that contributes to the misreading of the Book of Joshua as a story depicting a "conquest."

The first instance of the root *rhb* in the story of Noah governs the value of all other instances. An ark with the following dimensions, "three hundred cubits in length, fifty cubits in breadth (*rhb*), and thirty cubits in height,"[7] (Gen 6:15) can hardly be a place where all the earth animals and birds mentioned would fit (7:2-3, 8-9). So the intention is that the ark, just as the garden in Eden, is to function as God's entire earth, where all his creatures enjoy life in full togetherness. The next instance for the use of the root *rhb* is in a statement to Abram:

> The Lord said to Abram, after Lot had separated from him, "Lift up your eyes, and look from the place where you are, northward and southward and eastward and westward; for all the earth which you see I will give to you and to your descendants for ever. I will make your descendants as the dust of the earth; so that if one can count the dust of the earth, your descendants also can be counted. Arise, walk through the length and the breadth (*rohab*) of the earth, for I will give it to you." (Gen 13:14-17)

Two points are important in this passage. First, seeing as far as one can see from where one is standing, along with the invitation to walk the length and breadth of that earth, reflects Abraham's status as shepherd, and thus someone who sojourns that earth without owning any part of it. Secondly, the descendants of Abraham would include the progenies of Ishmael and Esau as well as those of Isaac and Jacob. Here again, we see the inclusiveness of all human beings living on the earth of God's

---

[7] A cubit is roughly the length of the human arm.

promise. Such inclusiveness is expressed in sharing, that is, in hospitality.

The third instance of the root *rḥb* is found in a story that relates the fate of utter destruction visited by God himself upon those living in Sodom and Gomorrah who did not hospitably share God's earth. What saved Lot from among all the inhabitants of Sodom was his hospitality:

> The two angels came to Sodom in the evening; and Lot was sitting in the gate of Sodom. When Lot saw them, he rose to meet them, and bowed himself with his face to the earth, and said, "My lords, turn aside, I pray you, to your servant's house and spend the night, and wash your feet; then you may rise up early and go on your way." They said, "No; we will spend the night in the open (*reḥob*)." But he urged them strongly; so they turned aside to him and entered his house; and he made them a feast, and baked unleavened bread, and they ate. (Gen 19:1-3)

Indeed, the two angels in question were close companions of the Lord himself and thus representatives of him (Gen 18:1-2). Sodom failed the test of hospitality that both Abraham and Lot passed. What is impressive in this story is that in it we already have the teaching that Matthew presents as the basis for the final judgment, care for the needy other in whatever circumstance: "Truly, I say to you, as you did it to one of the least of these my brethren, you did it to me. ... Truly, I say to you, as you did it not to one of the least of these, you did it not to me." (Mt 25:40, 45)

The clearest instance of the all-encompassing inclusiveness reflected in the root *rḥb* is linked to Isaac, the "perfect" being whom all are invited to emulate. After persevering in his peaceful attitude of not quarrelling with his presumed enemies who kept contending with him about the wells he would dig (Gen 26:19-21), Isaac was finally graced with a well that cemented the peace with the Philistines he was yearning for in the earth granted to him by God: "And he moved from there and dug another well, and over that they did not quarrel; so he called its name Rehoboth (*rehobot*), saying, 'For now the Lord has made room (*hirhib*; from the root *rhb*) for us, and we shall be fruitful in the earth.'" (v.22)

The last instance of *rhb* appears in conjunction with the odious sin committed by the sons of Jacob when they flagrantly used circumcision as guise to slaughter the inhabitants of Shechem, who welcomed Jacob's family: "These men are friendly with us; let them dwell in the land and trade in it, for behold, the earth is *large enough* (*rahab*) for them; let us take their daughters in marriage, and let us give them our daughters. Only on this condition will the men agree to dwell with us, to become one people: that every male among us be circumcised as they are circumcised." (Gen 34:21-22) The original text is very interesting, since the actual expression translated as "large enough" is *rahabat-yadayim* (wide the width of both hands). This is a phrase reflecting a full welcome made with both hands (or arms). Consequently, the text means that the inhabitants of Shechem *welcomed with open arms* the children of Jacob to share their earth with them. Yet, Jacob's sons used circumcision, the sign of the covenant of all-inclusiveness, to massacre the Shechemites!

The subsequent instance found in Exodus 3:8 is a judgment on the behavior of Jacob's sons toward the local resident Shechemites with whom they were supposed to share the earth: "I have come down to deliver them out of the hand of the

Egyptians, and to bring them up out of that earth to a good and broad (*reḥabah*) earth, an earth flowing with milk and honey, to the place of the Canaanites, the Hittites, the Amorites, the Perizzites, the Hivites, and the Jebusites."

All of this digression is to help understand what happened in the Book of Joshua. The entrance was not the "work" of the spies, nor the work of Israel; rather it was exclusively the "work" of God to instruct both the spies and Israel in the ways of Isaac. To use the terminology of Ezekiel, Rahab, the welcoming one, who was a harlot, extended a helping hand to the needy. This, subsequently, Israel will not do, and it is this lack of mercy that will be the reason for its demise:

> You [Jerusalem] are the daughter of your mother, who loathed her husband and her children; and you are the sister of your sisters [Samaria and Sodom], who loathed their husbands and their children. Your mother was a Hittite and your father an Amorite. And your elder sister is Samaria, who lived with her daughters to the north of you; and your younger sister, who lived to the south of you, is Sodom with her daughters. Yet you were not content to walk in their ways, or do according to their abominations; within a very little time you were more corrupt than they in all your ways. As I live, says the Lord God, your sister Sodom and her daughters have not done as you and your daughters have done. *Behold, this was the guilt of your sister Sodom: she and her daughters had pride, surfeit of food, and prosperous ease, but did not aid the poor and needy.* They were haughty, and did abominable things before me; therefore I removed them, when I saw it. (Ezek 16:45-50)

Through a shaming example performed, no less, by a "harlot," God sought to impose on Israel the sharing of the earth with its other inhabitants and even learning hospitality from them! However, the children of Israel, in their turn a "harlot" (Ezek 16 and 23), did not heed the lesson—they did not welcome the poor and the needy with open arms. Thus their end will be that of Sodom, the prime example of lack of hospitality.

That the author had this teaching in mind in his choice of the name Rahab is sealed in the following conversation between her and the spies:

> "Now then, swear to me by the Lord that as I have dealt kindly (did *ḥesed*) with you, you also will deal kindly (do *ḥesed*) with my father's house, and give me a sure sign (sign of *'emet*), and save alive my father and mother, my brothers and sisters, and all who belong to them, and deliver our lives from death." And the men said to her, "Our life for yours! If you do not tell this business of ours, then we will deal kindly and faithfully (do *ḥesed we'emet*) with you when the Lord gives us the land (earth)." (Josh 2:12-14)

The Hebrew *ḥesed* means "zealous care" and is translated as *eleos* (mercy; LXX); "mercy" (KJV); "love" (JB); and "steadfast love" (RSV). It is quintessentially a divine attribute in scripture as is evident especially in Psalm 136 where the phrase "for his [the Lord's] steadfast love (*ḥesed*) endures for ever" is heard in each of its twenty-six verses. In Joshua, not only are we told that Rahab exhibited such an attitude, but also Israel, through its spies, is to commit itself to do the same in Canaan, the land that the Lord is about to grant them. The seriousness of the matter is underscored through the repeated use of *'emet*. This Hebrew word connotes "truth, reality, indeed-ness" and is also another quintessential divine attribute in scripture referring specifically to God in conjunction with his activity as judge, which is par excellence the defining function of a deity. Unless the Israelites *truthfully* follow Rahab's behavior of *ḥesed*, they will pay with their own lives at God's hand, as did the Sodomites, their "cousins," who resided in Canaan. (Gen 19:23-29)

5

Final Instruction before the Crossing

The "Way" of the Lord

The preliminary comments regarding the entrance into Canaan are intended to establish firmly in the minds of the people that their leader in that venture is none save "the Lord your God." However, the Lord is not a deity represented in a statue and carried in a mobile tabernacle, but rather a deity whose presence is ensured through its will inscribed in the Book of the Law which was carried in "the ark of the covenant" by the Levitical priests (Josh 3:3). This view of the Lord is so essential that it was meant to remain the rule throughout the following centuries in the Kingdoms of Israel and Judah:

> When you come to the land which the Lord your God gives you, and you possess it and dwell in it, and then say, "I will set a king over me, like all the nations that are round about me"; you may indeed set as king over you him whom the Lord your God will choose. One from among your brethren you shall set as king over you; you may not put a foreigner over you, who is not your brother … And when he sits on the throne of his kingdom, he shall write for himself in a book a copy of this law, from that which is in the charge of the Levitical priests; and it shall be with him, and he shall read in it all the days of his life, that he may learn to fear the Lord his God, by keeping all the words of this law and these statutes, and doing them; that his heart may not be lifted up above his brethren, and that he may not turn aside from the commandment, either to the right hand or to the left; so that he may continue long in his kingdom, he and his children, in Israel. (Deut 17:14-15, 18-20)

It is in this "form" that the Lord will be with Joshua just as he was with Moses (Josh 3:7). That is why the invitation to follow this God is tantamount to following his "way," a way that the people did not know (v.4b) but is revealed to them through the divine law. It is abiding by its statutes that will secure their stay in Canaan. In scriptural terms, their being kept by God in the earth that is granted to them as inheritance is the other side of the coin of their keeping the commandments. The strictness of this matter is reflected in that the people are asked to "sanctify (*hitqaddašu*) yourselves; for tomorrow the Lord will do wonders among you" (v.5). The reason is that they are to be "holy" in the presence of the Holy One (*qadoš*). That the reference is to the Law rather than a so-called "personal" and thus statuesque God is evident in that one hears the same request in conjunction with the issuance of the Law by the God whom no one is allowed to see:

> *At the end of three days* the officers went through the camp and commanded the people, "When you see the ark of the covenant of the Lord your God being carried by the Levitical priests, then you shall set out from your place and follow it, that you may know the way you shall go, for you have not passed this way before. Yet there shall be a space between you and it, a distance of about two thousand cubits; do not come near it." And Joshua said to the people, "*Sanctify yourselves* (*hitqaddašu*); for tomorrow the Lord will do wonders among you." (Josh 3:2-5)

> And the Lord said to Moses, "Go to the people and *consecrate them* (*qiddaštem*) today and tomorrow, and let them wash their garments, and be ready *by the third day*; for *on the third day* the Lord will come down upon Mount Sinai in the sight of all the people. And you shall set bounds for the people round about, saying, 'Take heed that you do not go up into the mountain or touch the border of it; whoever touches the mountain shall be put

to death; no hand shall touch him, but he shall be stoned or shot; whether beast or man, he shall not live.' When the trumpet sounds a long blast, they shall come up to the mountain." So Moses went down from the mountain to the people, *and consecrated* (*wayqaddeš*) the people; and they washed their garments. And he said to the people, "Be ready *by the third day*; do not go near a woman." (Ex 19:10-15)

So the ark of the covenant, which hosts the Law, is as ominously unapproachable as the holy mountain where the same Law was delivered.

This is further confirmed in the enigmatic addition of "Yet there shall be a space between you and it, a distance of about two thousand cubits" (Josh 3:4b). As one learns later, the Levites are treated in a special way in that their heritage is apportioned out of the heritage of the other tribes in order to have them dispersed among the people as an ever reminder to all of the "presence" of the divine law among them (21:1-8). The Levitical cities, we are told, are to be surrounded by their "pasture lands" according to "the Lord's command through Moses" (vv.2-3). When one turns to that command one hears the following:

The Lord said to Moses in the plains of Moab by the Jordan at Jericho, "Command the people of Israel, that they give to the Levites, from the inheritance of their possession, cities to dwell in; and you shall give to the Levites pasture lands round about the cities. The cities shall be theirs to dwell in, and their pasture lands shall be for their cattle and for their livestock and for all their beasts. The pasture lands of the cities, which you shall give to the Levites, shall reach from the wall of the city outward a thousand cubits all round. And you shall measure, outside the city, for the east side two thousand cubits, and for the south side two thousand cubits, and for the west side two thousand cubits, and for the north side two thousand cubits, the city being in the middle; this shall belong to them as pasture land for their cities. The cities which you give to the Levites shall be the six cities of refuge, where you shall permit the manslayer to flee, and in addition to them you shall give forty-two cities. All the cities which you give to the Levites shall be forty-eight, with their pasture lands." (Num 35:1-7)

So the distance of two thousand cubits in Joshua 3:4b is an indication that the "sanctity" of the Law is of the same value as the sanctity of God himself. Put otherwise, the audible Law is tantamount to the invisible God; it is his exclusive tangible expression, the aim of which is to secure blessing and life for the people should they abide by its injunctions, rather than curse and death should they disobey its dictates (Josh 8:34; see also Lev 26; Deut 28; Ezek 18:23, 32; 33:11). The Law's protective function, reflecting God's *ḥesed* for the people, is evident in that the Levitical cities are part of the cities of refuge. These cities serve to protect those guilty by inadvertence (Num 35), a matter that will be revisited in Joshua 20:1-21:8. It is thus the Law, preserved in the ark of the covenant of the Lord, which protects those who follow its way (3:4a) and not vice-versa. Indeed, how could the people protect an ark when they are to maintain a distance of two thousand cubits between it and them?[1]

horiš *and* 'orišennu

Joshua 3:10 presents us with a good opportunity to unlock the true meaning of the causative *horiš* (the fifth verbal form of *yaraš* [inherit]), which is usually translated as "drive out." Such a translation is curious, to say the least, since the expected would be "make to inherit, give as inheritance." In Joshua 23:5 RSV

---

[1] This teaching concerning the ark as tantamount to the actual presence of God is revisited in the flowery lengthy series of episodes of 1 Sam 4-6.

reads: "The Lord your God will push them back before you, and drive them out (*horiš*) of your sight; and you shall possess (*yiraštem*; inherit) their land, as the Lord your God promised you." It is clearly a case of someone being disinherited while another is granted that same heritage by the one who has the power to do so. In a similar instance RSV actually translates *horiš* into "disinherit":

> And the Lord said to Moses, "How long will this people despise me? And how long will they not believe in me, in spite of all the signs which I have wrought among them? I will strike them with the pestilence and disinherit them (*'orišennu* from *horiš*), and I will make of you a nation greater and mightier than they." (Num 14:11-12)

Moses and those faithful around him, including Joshua (v.6), are promised the inheritance of the people who were dispossessed. The conclusion is unavoidable: the terminology of *horiš* has to do with assigning the heritage to someone instead of another.

But why not simply use the straightforward terminology of "giving" the heritage to someone who, in turn, would "inherit" (*yaraš*)? Why the stress on the disinheritance of another? The answer lies in that, in scripture, the heritage is given *conditionally*. The condition is that the heir is to abide by the will of the granter so that the inheritance would be preserved according to the latter's wishes. Unlike common human history, the scriptural heir never becomes the proprietor of the heritage; "the Lord (*yahweh*) alone is the master (*'adon*) of the earth" (Joshua 3:13) and its proprietor (*melek*) and remains so throughout the ages. All the heirs will have to prove worthy of the commission or else they would be disinherited. This motif runs like a crimson thread throughout scripture starting with the story of Adam who is placed in a garden that *the Lord God planted*; only Adam's unconditional obedience would secure that he remain there unharmed. The parallelism between Genesis 2 and Joshua is evidenced in that, in both cases, the earth is referred to as a place of *nuaḥ* (enjoyable rest):

> The Lord God took the man and put him (*wayyanniḥehu*; the fifth verbal form of *nuaḥ*) in the garden of Eden to till it and keep it. (Gen 2:15)

> Your wives, your little ones, and your cattle shall remain in the land which Moses gave you beyond the Jordan; but all the men of valor among you shall pass over armed before your brethren and shall help them, until the Lord gives rest (*yaniaḥ*; the fifth verbal form of *nuaḥ*) to your brethren as well as to you, and they also take possession of (*yaresu*; inherit) the land which the Lord your God is giving them; then you shall return to the land of your possession (*yerussah*; inheritance), and shall possess (*yeristem*; inherit) it, the land which Moses the servant of the Lord gave you beyond the Jordan toward the sunrise. (Josh 1:14-15)

As indicated earlier, the nations that had been dwelling in Canaan were disinherited because of their unrighteousness (Deut 9:4-6); the new heir "Israel" eventually will succumb to the same fate. Yet its punishment will be harsher and "more just (legal)" because Israel knew the Law that was expressly read to it (Josh 8:34-35).

That is why translating "the living God" as the agent of the action of disinheriting instead of the original "a living God" (Hebrew *'el ḥay*; Greek *theos zōn*) in 3:10 is as inaccurate as it is misleading. RSV's option is inexcusable given that it renders the same as "a living God" in 1 Thessalonians 1:9: "For they themselves report concerning us what a welcome we had among you, and how you turned to God from idols, to serve a living and true God." The scriptural God is not, based on a philosophical premise, the only deity. Even the sketchiest of glances at scripture will prove such a premise to be faulty; later, when Joshua will challenge the tribes to "opt" for the Lord whom he opted "for," he explained to them that such option entailed forsaking the "other gods" (24:14-24).[2] Rather the Lord has to show himself, in comparison with those "other gods," as indeed "a living God." And he will prove to be living, and thus effective, in his action of disinheriting the nations, in spite of the fact that he is not represented by a statue and thus does not seem to be "present." His presence is made manifest in the "wonders" he performs (Josh 3:5; see also Ps 72:18; 86:10; 98:1; 136:4), in this case allowing the people to cross the waterbed as a dry ground (Josh 3:13-18) just as he did at the Red Sea (Ex 4:15-15:21). The parallelism between these two stories is secured though the use of similar terminology: "heap" (*ned*; Ex 15:8: Josh 3:13, 16);[3] "doing wonders" (*'oseh phele'*; Ex 15:11) and "will do wonders" (*ya'aseh niphla'ot*; Josh 3:5); *ḥarabah* (dry land, Ex 15:19; dry ground, Josh 3:17 [twice]). The similarity in the action of leaving Egypt and entering Canaan is intentional. The first one was done to bring the people out of the predicament of the curse of slavery, in which they put themselves, in order to bring them to the mountain where they would hear the Law intended to secure life and blessing for them. This Law was laid in the ark of the covenant, which would lead another crossing into Canaan, and would be an ever reminder that only by keeping the divine commandments would

---

[2] See later my comments on that chapter.

[3] The other three instances of *ned* in the Hebrew text of the Old Testament are found in Is 17:11; Ps 33:7; 78:13, the last instance describing the exodus. In Is 17:11, RSV has "will flee away" instead of "*shall be* a heap." In Ps 33:7 RSV reads "as in a bottle," following the LXX, instead of "as an heap" (KJV).

the people be kept safe from the curse entailed in that Law. Otherwise, they would end up losing their inheritance and made to "return to Egypt" (Hos 8:13; 9:3, 6; 11:5), which is what will eventually happen. Canaan is intended as the earth of test as well as rest. This connection is evidenced in that the latter is closely linked to the "testing" Law:

> And when the soles of the feet of the priests who bear the ark of the Lord, the Lord of all the earth, shall rest (*noah*) in the waters of the Jordan, the waters of the Jordan shall be stopped from flowing, and the waters coming down from above shall stand in one heap. ... Take twelve men from the people, from each tribe a man, and command them, "Take twelve stones from here out of the midst of the Jordan, from the very place where the priests' feet stood, and carry them over with you, and lay them down (*hinnahtem*) in the place where you lodge tonight." ... And the men of Israel did as Joshua commanded, and took up twelve stones out of the midst of the Jordan, according to the number of the tribes of the people of Israel, as the Lord told Joshua; and they carried them over with them to the place where they lodged, and laid them down (*yannihum*) there. (Josh 3:13; 4:2-3, 8)

This understanding is sealed in the metaphoric vocabulary of 3:16: "the waters coming down from above stood and rose up in a heap far off, at Adam (*'adam*), the city that is beside (*missad*) Zarethan (*saretan*), and those flowing down toward the sea of the Arabah, the Salt Sea, were wholly cut off; and the people passed over opposite Jericho." Listening to it in the original one hears "at Adam, the city that is *from* (out of, away from) *the snare* (*missad* [*min sad*]) of *their affliction* (*saretan*)." So the "wonder" wrought by God of bringing the people out of their affliction in Egypt into the earth of Canaan would be a blessing for them should they consider Canaan a "ground" (*'adamah*) for every human being (*'adam*), including the "sojourner," to live on (8:33, 35; 20:9). The link to Egypt is unavoidable for someone who knows Hebrew since in the Hebrew language Egypt is the scripturally fabricated symbolic noun *miṣrayim* whose meaning is "from (out of) double (much) affliction." In other words, the exodus from Egypt on dry ground through the waters was an invitation to hear the Law; the entrance into Canaan on dry ground through the waters is an invitation to abide by that Law. This intention is clearly behind the choice of *ḥarabah* over *yabbašah* to speak of the "dry land" (Josh 3:17). *ḥarabah* is from the same root as the mountain Horeb (*ḥoreb*) where the Law was issued. The first instance of that name in Exodus 3:1 is *ḥorebah*.[4]

---

[4] One may explain the ending *ah* as the "old accusative" with the connotation of direction, the ultimate meaning being "to Horeb," which would fit the context. Such is reflected in RSV (and [Moses] came to Horeb, the mountain of God) and even more so in KJV (and [Moses] came to the mountain of God, *even* to Horeb). Still the similarity in sound is unmistakable and most probably intended.

6
The Passage through the Jordan

The passage through the Jordan is cast both formally and materially as a reminder to the hearers of the first passage through the waters at the Red Sea. Besides the terminology of "heap," "doing wonders," and "dry ground" referred to earlier, notice further the use of "memorial" (*zikkaron*; Josh 4:7) and "testimony" (*'edut*; 4:15) that are unique in Joshua. The first three occurrences of "memorial" in scripture are found in Exodus in conjunction with the exodus from Egypt, more specifically with the associated feasts of Passover (12:14) and of Unleavened Bread (13:9); in Joshua the passage through the Jordan culminates with the celebration of Passover (5:10). In the second instance in Exodus we hear that the teaching is to be commemorated to "your son" (Ex 13:8; compare with Josh 4:6), and the "memorial" is to be "between your eyes, that the law of the Lord may be *in your mouth*" (Ex 13:9; compare with Josh 1:8). The third instance of "memorial" is in conjunction with a victory of Joshua before the sun set, which is to be recorded in a book: "so his [Moses'] hands were steady until the going down of the sun (compare with Josh 10:12-13) And Joshua mowed down Amalek and his people with the edge of the sword. And the Lord said to Moses, 'Write this as a memorial in a book and recite it in the ears of Joshua, that I will utterly blot out the remembrance of Amalek from under heaven.'" (Ex 17:12b-14).[1]

---

[1] Compare with Josh 10:10-13: "And the Lord threw them into a panic before Israel, who slew them with a great slaughter at Gibeon, and chased them by the way of the ascent of Bethhoron, and smote them as far as Azekah and Makkedah. And as they fled before Israel, while they were going down the ascent of Bethhoron, the Lord threw down great stones from heaven upon them as far as Azekah, and they died; there were more who died because of the hailstones than the men of Israel killed with the sword.

Since "memorial" is not to be found in the Prior Prophets outside Joshua 4:7, its scriptural "trajectory" brackets the span between the first Passover feast and its first celebration in Canaan. It is as though the people are invited to "remember" that the Lord delivered on his promise to the fathers to take their children out of Egypt and bring them into Canaan. The entire trek between Exodus 12:4 and Joshua 4:7 is triggered by the first occurrence of the root *zkr* (whence *zikkaron*) in Exodus: "And God heard their groaning, and God remembered [*wayyizkor*] his covenant with Abraham, with Isaac, and with Jacob." (Ex 2:24) And since the "memorial" in Joshua is to remind the future generations of the crossing of the Jordan under the leadership of the ark of the covenant, which contains the book of the Law, those generations are to understand that their future in Canaan hinges on their abiding by those divine statutes, as will become evident at the end of chapter 8 (vv.30-35).

A closer look at the vocabulary describing the Jordan crossing will reveal that the author used another device to underscore that point. While both the Red Sea and its waters are said to have been "divided" (Ex 14:16, 21), we hear no less than four times that the waters of the Jordan were "cut off" (Josh 3:13,[2] 16; 4:7 [twice]). The original Hebrew is the passive form *nikrat* of the verb *karat* (cut, cut off). When one considers that the original Hebrew for "make a covenant" is "cut a covenant" (*karat berit*),

---

Then spoke Joshua to the Lord in the day when the Lord gave the Amorites over to the men of Israel; and he said in the sight of Israel, 'Sun, stand thou still at Gibeon, and thou Moon in the valley of Aijalon.' And the sun stood still, and the moon stayed, until the nation took vengeance on their enemies. Is this not written in the Book of Jashar? The sun stayed in the midst of heaven, and did not hasten to go down for about a whole day. There has been no day like it before or since, when the Lord hearkened to the voice of a man; for the Lord fought for Israel."
[2] RSV has in this case "stopped" whereas KJV follows the original and translates it into "cut off."

then one can surmise that the author wanted to insure that the hearers take seriously the fact that the ark leading the procession through the Jordan is the ark *of the covenant* that is binding the people to their God. Moreover, in the Book of the Law pertaining to that covenant, we hear repeatedly that anyone who breaks certain statutes will be "cut off" (*nikrat*) from the congregation and left to perish, starting with the ruling concerning the Feast of the Unleavened Bread (Ex 12:15, 19), which is introduced as a "memorial" (*zikkaron*; 13:9). It is practically impossible for the hearers of the original Hebrew to miss this underlying connection between the different connotations of *karat*.

The Ark of the Testimony

Turning to "testimony" (*'edut*), Joshua 4:15 accounts for its sole occurrence in the entire book. Just as "memorial" brackets the story beginning with the celebration of the first Passover in Egypt and its first celebration in Canaan, so also "testimony" brackets the story of the feeding of the people with manna. In Exodus 16:31-34 we learn of the first provision with manna in conjunction with "testimony" (*'edut*; v.34):

Now the house of Israel called its name manna; it was like coriander seed, white, and the taste of it was like wafers made with honey. And Moses said, "This is what the Lord has commanded: 'Let an omer of it be kept throughout your generations, that they may see the bread with which I fed you in the wilderness, when I brought you out of the land of Egypt.'" And Moses said to Aaron, "Take a jar, and put an omer of manna in it, and place it before the Lord, to be kept throughout your generations." As the Lord commanded Moses, so Aaron placed it before the testimony, to be kept.

On the other hand, in Joshua 5:10-12 we hear:

While the people of Israel were encamped in Gilgal they kept the passover on the fourteenth day of the month at evening in the plains of Jericho. And on the morrow after the passover, on that very day, they ate of the produce of the land, unleavened cakes and parched grain. And the manna ceased on the morrow, when they ate of the produce of the land; and the people of Israel had manna no more, but ate of the fruit of the land of Canaan that year.

The story of the manna spans the period between the first Passover described in Exodus 12:1-12, 21-28 and its first celebration in Canaan described in Joshua 5:10-12. The intentional link between the two stories is firmly established by the author's use of both "memorial" (4:7) and "testimony" (v. 16). In the latter case this is unmistakable since elsewhere in Joshua, both before and after 4:16, one hears exclusively of "the ark of the covenant." In order to figure out the express purpose of referring to the ark as "the ark of the testimony" (4:16) one ought to start with that the manna was to be "kept before it *throughout your generations.*" The reason behind such is revealed in Deuteronomy, which is the Book of the Law that is iterated to the first of those "generations" (5:1-22), in a passage that contains the last two instances of "manna" before Joshua 5:12:

All the commandment which I command you this day you shall be careful to do, that you may live and multiply, and go in and possess (inherit) the land which the Lord swore to give to your fathers.[3] And you shall remember all the way which the Lord your God has led you these forty years in the wilderness, that he might humble you, testing you to know what was in your heart, whether you would keep his commandments, or not. And he humbled you and let you hunger and fed you with manna, which you did not know, nor did your fathers know; that he might make you know

---

[3] Josh 1:6 recalls this verse.

that man does not live by bread alone, but that man lives by everything that proceeds out of the mouth of the Lord ... Take heed lest you forget the Lord your God, by not keeping his commandments and his ordinances and his statutes, which I command you this day: lest, when you have eaten and are full, and have built goodly houses and live in them, and when your herds and flocks multiply, and your silver and gold is multiplied, and all that you have is multiplied, then your heart be lifted up, and you forget the Lord your God, who brought you out of the land of Egypt, out of the house of bondage, who led you through the great and terrible wilderness, with its fiery serpents and scorpions and thirsty ground where there was no water, who brought you water out of the flinty rock, who fed you in the wilderness with manna which your fathers did not know, that he might humble you and test you, to do you good in the end ... And if you forget the Lord your God and go after other gods and serve them and worship them, I solemnly warn you this day that you shall surely perish. Like the nations that the Lord makes to perish before you, so shall you perish, because you would not obey the voice of the Lord your God. (Deut 8:1-3, 11-16, 19-20)

So the manna to be kept before the ark of the testimony (Ex 16:34) is to function as a test as to whether the people would abide by the Lord's commandments and thus "live by everything that proceeds out of his mouth." Hearing the text of Joshua in the original, one will notice that this is precisely the intention behind the apparently sudden mention of "testimony" in 4:16. The entire episode dealing with the passage of the Jordan (3:1-5:1) is studded with the verb *'abar* (cross, pass over, pass through) that is used no less than 23 times, not counting the preposition *'eber* (beyond, across; 5:1).[4] Later, when Israel is routed in its first attack against Ai (7:4-5), Joshua complains

---

[4] Fifteen times besides the instance in 5:1.

with the following words: "Alas, O Lord God, why hast thou *brought* this people *over* (*he'abarta*; the fifth [causative] form of *'abar*) the Jordan at all, to give us into the hands of the Amorites, to destroy us? Would that we had been content to dwell beyond (*'eber*) the Jordan!" (7:7) To this God replies:

> Arise, why have you thus fallen upon your face? Israel has sinned; they have *transgressed* (*'aberu*) my covenant which I commanded them; they have taken some of the devoted things; they have stolen, and lied, and put them among their own stuff. Therefore the people of Israel cannot stand before their enemies; they turn their backs before their enemies, because they have become a thing for destruction. I will be with you no more, unless you destroy the devoted things from among you. Up, sanctify the people, and say, "Sanctify yourselves for tomorrow; for thus says the Lord, God of Israel, 'There are devoted things in the midst of you, O Israel; you cannot stand before your enemies, until you take away the devoted things from among you. In the morning therefore you shall be brought near by your tribes; and the tribe which the Lord takes shall come near by families; and the family which the Lord takes shall come near by households; and the household which the Lord takes shall come near man by man. And he who is taken with the devoted things shall be burned with fire, he and all that he has, because he has *transgressed* (*'abar*) the covenant of the Lord, and because he has done a shameful thing in Israel.'" (vv.10-13)

The following and only other reference to "transgressing the covenant" is found on Joshua's lips in a passage that is aimed at "the following generations" and uses terminology reminiscent of Deuteronomy 8:19-20:

> And now I am about to go the way of all the earth, and you know in your hearts and souls, all of you, that not one thing has failed of all the good things which the Lord your God promised concerning you; all have come to pass for you, not one of them has failed. But

just as all the good things which the Lord your God promised concerning you have been fulfilled for you, so the Lord will bring upon you all the evil things, until he have destroyed you from off this good land which the Lord your God has given you, if you *transgress* (*'obrekem*) the covenant of the Lord your God, which he commanded you, and go and serve other gods and bow down to them. Then the anger of the Lord will be kindled against you, and you shall perish quickly from off the good land which he has given to you. (Josh 23:14-16)

Thus, the play on the root *'abar* corresponds to the play on the root *karat* discussed earlier in that both point in the same direction: it is *exclusively* the abiding by the divine law that secures Canaan as heritage throughout the generations. This is further corroborated by the trajectory of the topic of "fear" in Joshua, which parallels that of *'abar*. The phrase "fear of the Lord" is a staple of Deuteronomy where it is tantamount to obedience to the divine commandments.[5] After having been told in Joshua 4 that the "fear of the Lord" (v.24) is expressed through the fear of Joshua as well as of Moses (v.14),[6] the communicators of God's law to the people, that phrase disappears only to be heard again in the last chapter of the book in the context of another farewell speech by Joshua:

"Now therefore fear the Lord, and serve him in sincerity and in faithfulness; put away the gods which your fathers served beyond the River, and in Egypt, and serve the Lord. And if you be unwilling to serve the Lord, choose this day whom you will serve, whether the gods your fathers served in the region beyond the

---

[5] 4:10; 5:29; 6:2,13, 24; 8:6; 10:12; 13:4; 17:19; 28:58; 31:12-13.

[6] While RSV has "On that day the Lord exalted Joshua in the sight of all Israel; and they stood in awe of him, as they had stood in awe of Moses, all the days of his life," KJV follows the original more closely: "On that day the Lord magnified Joshua in the sight of all Israel; and they feared (*wayyir'u*) him, as they feared (*yare'u*) Moses, all the days of his life."

River, or the gods of the Amorites in whose land you dwell; but as for me and my house, we will serve the Lord." Then the people answered, "Far be it from us that we should forsake the Lord, to serve other gods; ... And the people said to Joshua, "Nay; but we will serve the Lord." ... And the people said to Joshua, "The Lord our God we will serve, and his voice we will obey." *So Joshua made a covenant with the people that day, and made statutes and ordinances for them at Shechem.* (Josh 24:14-16, 21, 24-25)

What is still impressive concerning "testimony" (4:16) when compared with "memorial" (v.7) is that, whereas the memorial just concludes with the first celebration of Passover in Canaan (5:10), the testimony not only concludes the manna story, but looks ahead to Israel's disastrous story in the earth of God's promise as consigned in the Prior Prophets, a story whose denouement is the demise of both kingdoms, first Israel and then Judah. Indeed, while "memorial" is not found after Joshua 4:7 in the rest of that section of scripture, "testimony" occurs twice more, in 2 Kings 11:12 and 17:15. The latter case is evident:

Then the king of Assyria invaded all the land and came to Samaria, and for three years he besieged it. In the ninth year of Hoshea the king of Assyria captured Samaria, and he carried the Israelites away to Assyria, and placed them in Halah, and on the Habor, the river of Gozan, and in the cities of the Medes. And this was so, because the people of Israel had sinned against the Lord their God, who had brought them up out of the land of Egypt from under the hand of Pharaoh king of Egypt, and had feared other gods and walked in the statutes of the nations whom the Lord drove out (disinherited) before the people of Israel, *and of the kings of Israel, which they had made* [7] ... and they [the children of

---

[7] In v.8 I am following KJV which is closer to the original. RSV reads "and walked in the customs of the nations whom the Lord drove out before the people of Israel, and in the customs which the kings of Israel had introduced."

Israel] served idols, of which the Lord had said to them, "You shall not do this." *Yet the Lord warned Israel and Judah* by every prophet and every seer, saying, "Turn from your evil ways and keep my commandments and my statutes, in accordance with all the law which I commanded your fathers, and which I sent to you by my servants the prophets." But they would not listen, but were stubborn, as their fathers had been, who did not believe in the Lord their God. They despised his statutes, and his covenant that he made with their fathers, and the warnings (*'edotaw*; his *testimonies* [KJV]) which he gave them.[8] They went after false idols, and became false, and they followed the nations that were round about them, concerning whom the Lord had commanded them that they should not do like them ... Therefore the Lord was very angry with Israel, and removed them out of his sight; none was left but the tribe of Judah only. *Judah also did not keep the commandments of the Lord their God, but walked in the statutes which Israel had made.*[9] And the Lord rejected all the descendants of Israel, and afflicted them, and gave them into the hand of spoilers, until he had cast them out of his sight. (17:5-8, 12-15, 18-20)

Two points are worthy of note. On the one hand, although the passage is specifically dealing with the fall of Samaria, the capital of the Kingdom of Israel, it nevertheless includes the Kingdom of Judah in the overall picture of divine judgment since Judah is already emulating Israel by committing the same kind of disobedience. On the other hand, at the end of v.8, we have a specific reference to the kings and the statutes they introduced, which are similar to those of the nations. This seems, at first

---

[8] The same criticism occurs once in the Latter Prophets on Jeremiah's lips: "It is because you burned incense, and because you sinned against the Lord and did not obey the voice of the Lord or walk in his law and in his statutes and in his testimonies (*'edotaw*), that this evil has befallen you, as at this day." (Jer 44:23)

[9] Here again I am following KJV. RSV reads "but walked in the customs which Israel had introduced."

sight, strange since later in v.19 we have the same thought concerning the entirety of Israel having contravened God's commandments by introducing its own statutes. This "addition" makes sense only in conjunction with the verse that contains the earlier reference to "testimony."

2 Kings 11:12 describes the enthronement of the infant Joash, son of King Ahaziah of Judah, in the following terms: "Then he [the priest Jehoiada] brought out the king's son, and put the crown (*nezer*) *upon him*, and gave him the testimony (*'edut*); and they proclaimed him king, and anointed him; and they clapped their hands, and said, 'Long live the king!'"[10] The *nezer* is clearly the royal crown or, at least, a royal headgear as is evident from the following passage:

> Then David said to the young man who told him, "How do you know that Saul and his son Jonathan are dead?" And the young man who told him said, "By chance I happened to be on Mount Gilboa; and there was Saul leaning upon his spear; and lo, the chariots and the horsemen were close upon him. And when he looked behind him, he saw me, and called to me. And I answered, 'Here I am.' And he said to me, 'Who are you?' I answered him, 'I am an Amalekite.' And he said to me, 'Stand beside me and slay me; for anguish has seized me, and yet my life still lingers.' So I stood beside him, and slew him, because I was sure that he could not live after he had fallen; and I took the crown (*nezer*) *which was on his head* and the armlet which was on his arm, and I have brought them here to my lord." Then David took hold of his clothes, and rent them; and so did all the men who were with him; and they mourned and wept and fasted until evening for Saul and for Jonathan his son and for the people of the Lord and for the

---

[10] See also the parallel 2 Chr 23:11: "Then he brought out the king's son, and put the crown (*nezer*) *upon him*, and gave him the testimony (*'edut*); and they proclaimed him king, and Jehoiada and his sons anointed him, and they said, 'Long live the king.'"

house of Israel, because they had fallen by the sword. (2 Sam 1:5-12)

The apparently unexpected addition of "testimony" (*'edut*) to "crown" (*nezer*) at Joash's coronation is best explained against the following mandate of Deuteronomy:

When you come to the land which the Lord your God gives you, and you possess it and dwell in it, and then say, "I will set a king over me, like all the nations that are round about me"; you may indeed set as king over you him whom the Lord your God will choose ... And when he sits on the throne of his kingdom, he shall write for himself in a book a copy (*mišneh*) of this law, from that which is in the charge of the Levitical priests; and it shall be with him, and he shall read in it all the days of his life, that he may learn to fear the Lord his God, by keeping all the words of this law and these statutes, and doing them; that his heart may not be lifted up above his brethren, and that he may not turn aside from the commandment, either to the right hand or to the left; so that he may continue long in his kingdom, he and his children, in Israel. (17:14-15a, 18-20)

According to Joshua the Book of the Law was carried into Canaan in the "ark of the covenant" by the Levitical priests in charge of it (3:33; 8:33). More specifically, in chapter 8 we hear the following:

And there, in the presence of the people of Israel, he wrote upon the stones a copy (*mišneh*) of the law of Moses, which he had written. And all Israel, sojourner as well as homeborn, with their elders and officers and their judges, stood on opposite sides of the ark before the Levitical priests who carried the ark of the covenant of the Lord, half of them in front of Mount Gerizim and half of them in front of Mount Ebal, as Moses the servant of the Lord had commanded at the first, that they should bless the people of Israel. And afterward he read all the words of the law, the blessing and the curse, according to all that is written in the book of the law. There was not a word of all that Moses commanded which Joshua did not read before all the assembly of Israel, and the women, and the little ones, and the sojourners who lived among them. (vv.32-35)

Given that the phrase "a copy (*mišneh*) of the law (of Moses)" occurs in scripture only in the preceding two instances, their connection is clearly deliberate. It is this passage in Joshua that explains how the "testimony" eventually reached the temple and subsequently was used at the coronation ceremonies (2 Kg 11:12). In turn, the function of 2 Kings 17:15 is intended to show how the kings failed miserably to abide by the mandate of Deuteronomy and, in so doing, precipitated the just demise of their kingdom.

Thus, when Joshua is read as it should be, i.e., as a ring in the chain that hinges two scriptural parts, the Law and the Prophets, it ceases to be a Jewish-Christian crusade of a triumphant military conquest. Rather it is a work that prepares for as well as introduces the calamitous story of how Israel was invited to inherit Canaan, yet lost that heritage due to its stubborn disobedience to the divine commandments of the Law. This view is already reflected in the magisterially devised passages that ends the "crossing of the Jordan":

The people came up out of the Jordan on the tenth day of the first month, and they encamped in Gilgal on the east border of Jericho. And those twelve stones, which they took out of the Jordan, Joshua set up in Gilgal. And he said to the people of Israel, "When your children ask their fathers in time to come, 'What do these stones mean?' then you shall let your children know, 'Israel passed over this Jordan on dry ground.' For the Lord your God dried up the waters of the Jordan for you until you passed over, as the Lord your God did to the Red Sea, which he dried up for us until we passed over, so that all the peoples of the earth may know that the hand of the Lord is mighty; that you may fear the Lord your God for ever." When all the kings of the Amorites that were beyond the Jordan to the west, and all the kings of the Canaanites that were by the sea, heard that the Lord had dried up the waters of the Jordan for the people of Israel until they had crossed over, their heart melted, and there was no longer any spirit in them, because of the people of Israel. (Josh 4:19-5:1)

The first verse is studded with allusions to the resolution of the story in the punishment of exile, which is precisely what we found in discussing the meteoric introduction of "testimony" four verses earlier (4:15). Gilgal is explained later on the basis of the verb *galah* meaning "roll away" (5:9) and thus "uncover, denude, bare" and, ultimately, "send into exile" a city left bare and empty.[11] This Gilgal is furthermore said to be "on the east border of Jericho," the city where Israel's sin of very early disobedience is about to be unveiled (7:10-26). This interest in Israel's sin of disobedience that led to the exile is further reflected in the mention of the first day of the month (4:19), which looks ahead to the reference to the first celebration of Passover in Canaan on the fourteenth day of the month (5:10). Indeed, ironically one does not hear of Passover again until 2 Kings 23, and no less in the following negative terms:

And the king commanded all the people, "Keep the passover to the Lord your God, as it is written in this book of the covenant."

---

[11] See, e.g., "the captivity (*gelut*) of Jerusalem" (Jer 1:3); see also Ezek 12:3: "*go into exile (geleh)* in their sight; you shall *go like an exile (galita)* from your place to another place in their sight"; and also Ezek 39:23: "And the nations shall know that the house of Israel *went into captivity (galu)* for their iniquity, because they dealt so treacherously with me that I hid my face from them and gave them into the hand of their adversaries, and they all fell by the sword."

For no such passover had been kept since the days of the judges who judged Israel, or during all the days of the kings of Israel or of the kings of Judah; but in the eighteenth year of King Josiah this passover was kept to the Lord in Jerusalem. (vv.21-23)

In other words, Israel's foolish loss of the heritage was due to its having betrayed the "memorial" of the exodus. This thought is further underscored in the way the rest of the passage (Josh 4:19-5:1) is construed. The "memorial" that is to be relayed to the upcoming children (4:5-7) consists in likening the crossing of the waters "on dry ground" into Canaan to the crossing of the waters "on dry ground" through the Red Sea (vv.21-23) with the intention of showing the nations the might of God's hand (4:24a and 5:1) just as it was shown to Pharaoh (Ex 3:19-20; 15:6, 9, 12). However, this show of might is merely a "show" for the nations. The real lesson is for Israel: "that you may fear the Lord your God for ever." (Josh 4:24b) And this is precisely what Israel will not do: fear the Lord by keeping his commandments. That is why, just as the crossing of the Red Sea was followed by the fathers' disobedience in the wilderness, the crossing of Jordan will result in their children's disobedience in Canaan—"like mother, like daughter" (Ezek 16:44b): "Son of man, I send you to the people of Israel, to a nation of rebels, who have rebelled against me; they and their fathers have transgressed against me to this very day." (2:3) Gilgal was supposed to "roll away" the "reproach of Egypt"; instead Jerusalem ended up "rolled away into exile" and, as such, an "object of reproach" for the nations (5:14, 15; 16:57; 22:4).

7

Circumcision and the Celebration of Passover

In view of the celebration of Passover (Josh 5:10) and considering the statute governing it that "no uncircumcised person shall eat of it" (Ex 12:44b), Joshua had to first circumcise the entire congregation since "all the people that were born on the way in the wilderness after they had come out of Egypt had not been circumcised" (Josh 5:5b; see also v.7). Through a series of literary devices, the author takes this opportunity to remind the hearers that the heritage is not to be taken for granted. First of all, circumcision is no guarantee for inheritance.[1] The circumcised Israelites who left Egypt perished in the wilderness because "they did not hearken to the voice of the Lord; to them the Lord swore that he would not let them see the land which the Lord had sworn to their fathers to give us, a land flowing with milk and honey" (v.6b). Notice further how the disobedient people are purposely referred to as a "nation" (*goy*; v.6a),[2] that is to say, on par with the nations that are about to be disinherited because of their wickedness (Deut 9:3-6). The lesson for the newly circumcised is unmistakable: only obedience to God's will as inscribed in his law can ensure hope that the divine promise will be honored. Secondly, in the Hebrew original the attention of the hearer has already been incited by the location startlingly named Gibeath-haaraloth (5:3). The Hebrew *gib'at ha'aralot*

---

[1] Paul will later remind the Galatians of this scriptural truth.

[2] See Ezek 2:3 for a similar instance: "Son of man, I send you to the people of Israel, to a nation of rebels, who have rebelled against me; they and their fathers have transgressed against me to this very day."

119

means "the mound of the foreskins." On the one hand, *gib'ah*[3] (mound) is a reminder of *tel*, another term for mound, but indicating a heap of rubble. Though circumcised, Israel may well turn out into a "heap of ruins" as Ai turned out to be—"So Joshua burned Ai, and made it for ever a heap (*tel*) of ruins, as it is to this day" (8:28)—even though the inhabitants of Ai first routed Israel and brought it to the verge of extinction (7:5). Put otherwise, the circumcised Israelites in Canaan were in no better condition than their fathers in the wilderness. On the other hand, and more importantly, the term *gib'ah* was chosen in view of chapters 9 and 10 where Joshua and the elders are lured into a covenant of peace with the inhabitants of *gib'on* (Gibeon). A covenant, even with an uncircumcised, is still a covenant and may not be broken at any cost. After all, when the Lord decided to enter into a covenant with Abraham, the latter was still uncircumcised (Gen 17) and thus still like the "nations" (Rom 4:9-12).

The combination of these two features concerning circumcision leads to the conclusion that fleshly circumcision on its own ends up as a dry heap of rubble if it is not seasoned with the circumcision of the heart, that is to say, strict adherence to God's will. That is precisely what Deuteronomy has already taught the hearers: "Circumcise therefore the foreskin of your heart, and be no longer stubborn" (10:16); "And the Lord your God will circumcise your heart and the heart of your offspring, so that you will love the Lord your God with all your heart and with all your soul, that you may live." (30:6)

The episode of theophany at the end of Joshua 5 (vv.13-15) seals what we have found all along concerning the author's

---

[3] *gib'ah* changes into *gib'at* when followed by a noun complement.

interest in bringing the two "crossings" into close parallelism. Notice that the leader of the crossing out of Egypt was not Moses, but the Lord himself (Ex 15:1-21); so also here the leader is not Joshua but the commander of the Lord's army. Moreover, at Joshua's encounter with the commander of the Lord's army, he is asked to "put off your shoes from your feet; for the place where you stand is holy" (Josh 5:15), just as Moses had to do when he faced the Lord (Ex 3:5). Finally, one should add, that the Hebrew noun rendered as "adversaries" (Josh 5:13) is *ṣarim*, plural of *ṣar*. Elsewhere in the book we find repeatedly the noun *'oyeb* (enemy, adversary; 7:8, 12 [twice]; 13; 10:13, 19, 25; 21:44 [twice]; 22:8; 23:1). Given that there is only one other instance of *ṣar* in the Prior Prophets (2 Sam 24:13) whereas *'oyeb* is a staple of that literature, the choice of the former must have been intentional in that it is from the same root as *ṣarah* (affliction) found in *miṣrayim* (Egypt), a matter discussed earlier in conjunction with *ṣaretan* (Zarethan; Josh 3:16).

8

The Fall of Jericho

The "fall of Jericho" is the quintessential story of how the entrance into Canaan is exclusively the work of the Lord, done not only according to his own will toward Israel, but also toward all nations. Both Israel and the nations, represented in Rahab and her kinsfolk, are the recipients of God's gift of the earth where they would live under his beneficent yoke. The procession into Canaan is described with phraseology similar to that occurring elsewhere in conjunction with the people approaching the "holy" mountain of God (Ex 19:9-25). The verb *mašak* (stretch, draw out) is found exclusively in Exodus and Joshua where we even find the same phraseology of "at the blowing of the trumpet": *bimšok hayyobel* (Ex 19:13) and *bimšok ... hayyobel* (Josh 6:5). Moreover, it is only in these two passages in the entire scripture that the noun *yobel*, whose technical meaning is "jubilee" (see Lev 25 passim), is used to refer to the *šophar* (trumpet, ram's horn used as a trumpet). Consequently, just as the theophany to Moses, underscoring the holiness of the mountain (Ex 3:5), prepared the people to approach it with awe (19:9-25), similarly the theophany to Joshua (Josh 5:13-15) functions to remind the people that the earth of heritage they are about to step into is "holy" ground that is the exclusive property of God.

Although Joshua 6:1-16 is cast in Exodus 16 terminology, it nevertheless harks back to Leviticus 25 that speaks essentially of the jubilee year when individuals as well as land are liberated so that "the earth and all those who dwell therein" become "the Lord's" (Ps 24:1). Consider the following:

1. In Exodus we hear of the "third day" (19:11, 15, 16), however, it is the numeral seven that pervades Joshua 6 as much as it does Leviticus 25, which numeral is connected to the sabbatical and jubilee years.

2. The directives concerning the sabbatical and jubilee years are introduced with "Say to the people of Israel, When you come into the land (earth) which I give you, the land (earth) shall keep a sabbath to the Lord" (Lev 25:2), which corresponds to the beginning of Joshua (6:1-16).

3. In the jubilee year every inhabitant of the earth of Canaan is entitled to return to his 'ahuzzah ([inherited] property; Lev 25:10, 13, 25, 27, 28) just as the tribes in Joshua are entitled to their 'ahuzzah ([inherited] possession; Josh 21:12, 41; 22:4, 9, 19) as well as their inheritance (nahalah or yerussah).

4. In Leviticus 25 the many instances of the noun yobel systematically refer to the jubilee year.[1] The noun sophar is used twice in v.9—and only there in the entire book—to speak specifically of the trumpet made usually of ram's horn. In Joshua 6 we find the sole instances of these two nouns, yobel and sophar, in that book. So it stands to reason to surmise that the author's intention is to describe the entrance into Canaan and the fall of Jericho in terms of the jubilee year. The surmise

---

[1] The same applies to the six occurrences of yobel in Lev 27 (vv.17, 18 [twice], 21, 23, 24).

turns into factuality when the hearers realize that four of the ten occurrences of *šophar* in that chapter are part of the peculiar phrase *šopharot (hay)yobelim* ([the] trumpets of [the] jubilees; vv.4, 6, 8, 13). It is no wonder that RSV as well as KJV and JB translations are at a loss and render *šopharot (hay)yobelim* into "trumpets of ram's horns,"[2] thus unwarrantedly rendering "jubilee" here as a "ram's horn." The only instance of horn in the entire book occurs in v.5 as part of the phrase *qeren hayyobel* (the horn of the jubilee) that is translated as simply "ram's horn," which is how *yobel* by itself is rendered elsewhere. However, if one understands *qeren hayyobel*, as it should be understood, that is, as "the horn used at the jubilee," everything begins to make sense. The original v.5 explicates *qeren hayyobel* as being the *šophar*, which is precisely what one learns from Leviticus 25: "And when they make a long blast with *qeren hayyobel*, (that is to say), as soon as you hear the sound of *haššophar*, then all the people shall shout with a great shout; and the wall of the city will fall down flat, and the people shall go up every man straight before him." (Josh 6:5) Notice how *šophar* is both in the singular and with the definite article (*haššophar*). The same combination of *haššophar* and the city's wall falling down flat recurs at the end of the story (Josh 6:20), thus confirming the realization of

---

[2] KJV and JB have the singular "horn," which does not reflect the plural of the original Hebrew *yobelim*.

the divine prediction at the beginning (v.5). Put otherwise, although one hears repeatedly of (seven) trumpets in the passage, when it comes to the actual effect of those, one is suddenly faced not with those trumpets, but with *the* trumpet (v.20) that was introduced as "*the* horn of the jubilee" (v.5). So one can safely conclude that the blast of the seven trumpets, seven times around the city, for the period of seven days is a literary device to seal in the hearer's mind that the procession into Canaan is that of the jubilee year when all the earth pertains to each and every one dwelling on it. Furthermore, in order for one to remain unharmed on that earth, one's sins will have had to be purged on the Day of Atonement when all the earth and those who dwell on it will be atoned for and thus made "holy" (Lev 16) because "the place where you stand is holy" (Josh 5:15). Notice how the Leviticus phraseology concerning the sounding of the *šophar* on the Day of Atonement of the jubilee year literally as well as literarily "foresees" the Book of Joshua:

> And you shall count seven weeks of years, seven times seven years, so that the time of the seven weeks of years shall be to you forty-nine years. Then you shall send abroad (*ha'abarta* [2nd person singular of the fifth causative form of the verb *'abar*]; you shall make pass through [go across]) the loud trumpet (*šophar*)[3] on the tenth day of the

---

[3] The original Hebrew for "loud trumpet" is *šophar teru'ah*, which means "a trumpet of clamor (alarm, shout)." Compare with Josh 6:5: "And when they make a long blast

seventh month; on the day of atonement you shall send abroad (*ta'abiru* [2nd person plural of the fifth causative form of the verb *'abar*]; you shall make pass through [go across]) the trumpet (*šophar*) throughout all your land.[4] And you shall hallow (*qiddaštem*; sanctify)[5] the fiftieth year, and proclaim liberty throughout the land to all its inhabitants; it shall be a jubilee for you, when each of you shall return to his property (*'aḥuzzah*) and each of you shall return to his family (*mišpaḥah*; clan, village).[6] A jubilee shall that fiftieth year be to you; in it you shall neither sow, nor reap what grows of itself, nor gather the grapes from the undressed vines. For it is a jubilee; it shall be holy (*qodeš*) to you; you shall eat what it yields out of the field. In this year of jubilee each of you shall return to his property (*'aḥuzzah*). (Lev 25:8-13)

That the author had in mind the jubilee year, when the entire earth of Canaan is declared as the exclusive property of God, is corroborated in the rest of Joshua 6. First we hear of the dooming of Jericho to the *ḥerem* devoted or dedicated exclusively

---

with the horn of the *yobel*, (that is to say), as soon as you hear the sound of the *šophar*, then all the people shall *shout* (*yari'u*; a verb from the same root as *teru'ah*) with a great *shout* (*teru'ah*); and the wall of the city will fall down flat, and the people shall go up every man straight before him."

[4] Notice the intentional repetition, once in the singular and once in the plural, of the verb *he'ebir* the fifth causative form of the verb *'abar* (go through, cross, pass over) as well as of *šophar*. Notice further that, in both cases, the original Hebrew has *šophar* without the definite article whereby the meaning is "a," and thus "one," *šophar*.

[5] Compare with Josh 3:5: "And Joshua said to the people, 'Sanctify yourselves (*hitqaddašu*); for tomorrow the Lord will do wonders among you.'"

[6] These two Hebrew nouns are encountered profusely in Joshua.

to the Lord (6:17; 7:13) and, by the same token, is taboo to anyone else. The result as well as the intention of war is the spoil; normally speaking, it would be silly to wage a war and come out of it "empty handed." By decreeing a conquered city as *ḥerem*, the Lord is affirming that all its contents are his personal "spoil." The people are precisely to remain "empty handed" after the conquest: "Then they utterly destroyed all in the city, both men and women, young and old, oxen, sheep, and asses, with the edge of the sword" (6:21); "But all silver and gold, and vessels of bronze and iron, are sacred to the Lord; they shall go into the treasury of the Lord" (v.19); "And they burned the city with fire, and all within it; only the silver and gold, and the vessels of bronze and of iron, they put into the treasury of the house of the Lord." (v.24) By announcing that Jericho, the first city in Canaan to fall, was designated by God as *ḥerem* (v.17), Joshua was reminding the people that all that lives or is found on the earth they were entering was God's property. It can never become theirs to do with as they please. In other words, they were not to take advantage of that earth or anything that lives on it or is found in it. That earth is under God's aegis and protection, and he deals with it *as he pleases*. A clear indication of this intention can be seen in that Joshua's command regarding the *ḥerem* excluded Rahab and her relatives since they were protected by an oath taken before the Lord (2:14). Furthermore, any infraction of a declared *ḥerem* will cost its perpetrators to be doomed to *ḥerem*, that is to say, to be anathematized unto total destruction:

> And at the seventh time, when the priests had blown the trumpets, Joshua said to the people, "Shout; for the Lord has given you the city." And the city and all that is within it shall be devoted (*ḥerem*) to the Lord for destruction; only Rahab the harlot and all who are

with her in her house shall live, because she hid the messengers that we sent. But you, keep yourselves from *the things devoted to destruction* (*ḥerem*), lest when you have devoted (*teḥarimu*; from the same root as *ḥerem*) them you take any of *the devoted things* (*ḥerem*) and make the camp of Israel *a thing for destruction* (*ḥerem*), and bring trouble upon it. (6:16-18)

The preservation of Rahab is given prominence in an extensive passage (vv.22-25) which underscores that she, "the harlot," and her entire clan in Canaan were granted the same kind of "rest" (v.23) as the Israelite tribes,[7] and that they were still dwelling (*tešeb*; from the verb *yašab*) "in (the midst of)[8] Israel *to this day*." In other words, a harlot is as much welcome in the Lord's earth as those who have been "sanctified," since the Lord stated earlier in conjunction with the jubilee year: "The land shall not be sold in perpetuity, for the land is mine; for you are strangers (*gerim*; sojourners) and sojourners (*tošabim* from the root *yašab*; dwellers) with me." (Lev 25:24) The Gospel stories about Jesus sharing table fellowship with publicans and sinners as well as Pharisees will follow suit.

Finally, as an ever reminder for all subsequent generations of the divine prerogative to issue a *ḥerem* over any city the chapter ends with the following caveat: "Joshua laid an oath upon them at that time, saying, 'Cursed before the Lord be the man that rises up and rebuilds this city, Jericho. At the cost of his firstborn shall he lay its foundation, and at the cost of his youngest son shall he set up its gates.'" (Josh 6:26) Later in the Prior Prophets, the hearer is reminded of this curse: "And Ahab made

---

[7] The Hebrew for "set them" is *yanniḥum* that is the same causative fifth form of the verb *nuaḥ*, which occurs in 1:13, 15; 21:44; 22:4; and 23:1 in conjunction with the Lord's giving "rest" to the Israelite tribes in their heritages.

[8] The Hebrew has *beqereb* (in the midst of).

an Asherah. Ahab did more to provoke the Lord, the God of Israel, to anger than all the kings of Israel who were before him. In his days Hiel of Bethel built Jericho; he laid its foundation at the cost of Abiram his first-born, and set up its gates at the cost of his youngest son Segub, according to the word of the Lord, which he spoke by Joshua the son of Nun." (1 Kg 16:33-34) The function of the caveat is to prepare for the most severe judgment against the contravener of the *ḥerem*, whose sin will bring disaster on Israel.

9

The Sin of Achan

The Defeat at Ai

In order to explain the unexpected defeat of Israel by the residents of Ai (7:2-5), the author prefaces that story with a verse indicating that the *ḥerem* the Lord had issued regarding Jericho was breached: "But the people of Israel broke faith in regard to the devoted things (*ḥerem*); for Achan the son of Carmi, son of Zabdi, son of Zerah, of the tribe of Judah, took some of the devoted things (*ḥerem*); and the anger of the Lord burned against the people of Israel." (v.1) This accusation is aimed at the tribe of Judah and, by extension, the Kingdom of Judah whose capital, Jerusalem, will be doomed at the end of the overarching story covered in the Prior Prophets. So the author's intention is to point out that the sin of Judah and Jerusalem goes back to the earliest period of the entrance into Canaan; later the kings and the people under them will follow in the path of disobedience that will arouse the anger of the Lord and bring about the final doom. Still, such would have warranted a simple "Achan of the tribe of Judah"; yet there are three other intervening names. The only name that could be accounted for is Zerah, Judah's son (Gen 38:30); however, the question that arises is why Zerah, and not Perez (v.29) whose sons are Judah's only grandsons (46:12). Before Joshua 7 there is no mention of any Zabdi and the only Carmi we hear of is a son of Reuben, not Judah (Gen 46:9). Consequently, the three names in Achan's ascendancy are obviously metaphorical. The Hebrew *karmi* means "my vineyard" and occurs twice on the Lord's lips to speak of the sinful Jerusalem, Judah's capital (Is 5:3) and of its punishment at God's hand (Jer 12:10). The Hebrew *zabdi* means "my generous gift," which fully reflects what the Lord did for Jerusalem (Is 5:1-2; Jer 12:7).[1] Finally, the Hebrew verb *zarah* means "rise, shine forth (as the sun would)"[2] and thus would prefigure the rise to power of David, King of Judah. Since we have noticed that the Book of Joshua is a metaphorical series of stories foreshadowing the future sin of disobedience of the Kingdoms of Israel and Judah, then it stands to reason to consider the symbolic value of the names of Achan's forefathers and to view his flagrant infraction and punishment as a prefiguration of Jerusalem's iniquity and its demise. Remains for us to explain the choice of the Hebrew name *'akan*.

Since the root *'kn* is not extant in scripture, the function of *'akan* (Josh 7:1) seems to unravel in the resolution of the story:

> And Joshua and all Israel with him took Achan (*'akan*) the son of Zerah, and the silver and the mantle and the bar of gold, and his sons and daughters, and his oxen and asses and sheep, and his tent, and all that he had; and they brought them up to the Valley of Achor (*'akor*). And Joshua said, "Why did you bring trouble on us (*'akartanu*; from the verb *'akar*)? The Lord brings trouble on you (*ya'korka*) today." And all Israel stoned him with stones; they burned them with fire, and stoned them with stone. And they raised over him a great heap of stones that remains to this day; then the Lord turned from his burning anger. Therefore to this day the name of that place is called the Valley of Achor (*'akor*). (vv.24-26)

It is evident that the punishment of Achan revolves around a word play on the root *'kr* whose first two letters (consonants) are the same as the first two of the trilateral *'kn* (Achan). This is

---

[1] In Jer 12:7 Jerusalem is referred to as the Lord's "heritage" (*nahalah*).

[2] See, e.g. Gen 32:31; Ex 22:3; Judg 9:33; 2 Sam 23:4; 2 Kg 3:22.

precisely how the Chronicler understood the matter when he
changed the name from Achan to Achar in conjunction with
presenting him as the "troubler of Israel":

> Did not Achan (*'akan*) the son of Zerah break faith (*ma'al*) in the
> matter of the devoted things (*baherem*), and wrath fell upon all the
> congregation of Israel? And he did not perish alone for his
> iniquity. (Josh 22:20)[3]

> The sons of Carmi: Achar (*'akar*), the troubler (*'oker*; nominal
> active participle of *'akar*) of Israel, who transgressed (*ma'al*) in the
> matter of the devoted thing (*baherem*); and Ethan's son was
> Azariah. (1 Chr 2:7-8)

With patience hearers will be rewarded when they encounter the
only other instance of "troubler of Israel" in scripture in
conjunction with Elijah's criticism of Achab, one of the kings of
Israel who "rose" (*zarah*) to power and considered himself the
proprietor of the earth and its inhabitants, just as David did:[4]
"When Ahab saw Elijah, Ahab said to him, 'Is it you, you
troubler (*'oker*) of Israel?' And he answered, 'I have not troubled
(*'akarti*) Israel; but you have, and your father's house, because
you have forsaken the commandments of the Lord and followed
the Baals.'" (1 Kg 18:16-17)

Still, why *'akan* and not forthrightly *'akar*? The choice of the
former serves the express purpose of showing that, just as the

---

[3] Compare with Josh 7:1: "But the people of Israel broke faith (*yim'alu ma'al*) in
regard to the devoted things (*baherem*); for Achan the son of Carmi, son of Zabdi, son
of Zerah, of the tribe of Judah, took some of the devoted things; and the anger of the
Lord burned against the people of Israel."
[4] Compare the story of Achab and Naboth's vineyard (1 Kg 21) with David's behavior
toward Uriah and his wife Bathsheba (2 Sam 11:1-12:15). As a reminder, the Hebrew
root *mlk*, whence *melek* (king), has the connotation of "ownership, proprietorship,
possession."

entrance into the earth of heritage is a common endeavor (Josh 1:12-15), so is the punishment collective even in case of an individual infraction. The proof is that, when revisiting the entire relationship between the Cis-Jordan and the Trans-Jordan tribes (Josh 22), the fear that an infraction by the latter would affect the former is brought up in the following terms where reference is made to the entire Achan incident as a precedent: "But now, if your land is unclean, pass over into the Lord's land where the Lord's tabernacle stands, and take for yourselves a possession among us; only do not rebel against the Lord, or *make us as rebels* by building yourselves an altar other than the altar of the Lord our God. Did not Achan the son of Zerah break faith in the matter of the devoted things, and wrath fell upon all the congregation of Israel? And *he did not perish alone for his iniquity.*" (vv.19-20) Bearing this in mind, one will notice that the topic introduced in Joshua 7:1 is actually not Achan's sin, but rather the breaking of faith by the children of Israel.[5] Achan's infraction is an explanation of how such wickedness happened. In this regard, the choice of 'akan becomes understandable: the Hebrew ending *an* means "their" and thus the hearer is perceiving that the children committed a detrimental action whose first syllable is 'ak.[6] A careful listener will have guessed that the intended is 'akor since the beginning of the verse (But the children of Israel broke faith in regard to the devoted things [herem]) recalls terminology wise the caveat issued a few verses earlier concerning the eventual punishment of the entire "camp of Israel": "But you, keep yourselves from the things devoted to destruction (herem), lest when you have devoted them (taharimu) you take any of the devoted things (herem) and make

---

[5] RSV has "the people of Israel."

[6] Besides, the ending *an* (their) contrasts with the ending *i* (my) in *karmi* (my vineyard) and *zabdi* (my generous gift).

the camp of Israel a thing for destruction (*ḥerem*), and *bring trouble* (*'akartem*) upon *it*." (6:18) For those who will have missed the connection, it will be made clear to them at the end of the chapter when the anger of the Lord, promised in 7:1, is unleashed in v.26 and is cast in terms of "trouble" (*'akor*) on all of "us" (v.25). The alternate clearer choice *'akoran* instead of the shortened *'akan* would have been a tri-syllabic name that would have contrasted with the following dy-syllabic names *karmi*, *zabdi*, and *zeraḥ*.

Prelude to Punishment

For the keen ear, the introductory verse (7:2) to the story of Ai, the second city of Canaan to eventually fall, is a clear set up for the immediately following disaster. The Hebrew *'ay* means "ruin"; the stress on that meaning is betrayed in that the name of the city in the original is *ha'ay* with the definite article, the result being that we are told that Joshua sent men to spy on "the ruin"! Ai is further defined as being "near (with) Bethaven," the Hebrew *bet 'awen* meaning "the house of evil (mischief)," thus inviting the hearer to realize that the ruin was the outcome of an evil that was perpetrated and preparing the way for the end of the chapter when the anger of the Lord will strike the evildoer. Finally, and perhaps most importantly, Ai is said to be "(on the) east of Bethel" (*miqqedem lebet 'el*), a phrase that occurs verbatim in scripture only once more: "Thence he [Abram] removed to the mountain on the east of Bethel (*miqqedem lebet 'el*), and pitched his tent, with Bethel on the west and Ai (*ha'ay*) on the east; and there he built an altar to the Lord and called on the name of the Lord." (Gen 12:8) One cannot miss the intended contrast between the story of Abraham and that of his children who were about to inherit the earth of Canaan *according to the promise* made to their forefather:

And Abram took Sarai his wife, and Lot his brother's son, and all their possessions which they had gathered, and the persons that they had gotten in Haran; and they set forth to go to the land of Canaan. When they had come to the land of Canaan, Abram passed through the land to the place at Shechem, to the oak of Moreh. At that time the Canaanites were in the land. Then the Lord appeared to Abram, and said, "To your descendants I will give this land." So he built there an altar to the Lord, who had appeared to him. Thence he removed to the mountain on the east of Bethel, and pitched his tent, with Bethel on the west and Ai on the east; and there he built an altar to the Lord and called on the name of the Lord. (vv.5-8)

In spite of their cocky assuredness (Josh 7:3) the Israelites will flounder at the same spot where their forefather pitched his tent and firmly established a dwelling for himself and his own family without an army! This dwelling was the haven Abram would come back to after his calamitous escapade into Egypt "due to a famine in the land" (Gen 12:10–13:1): "And he journeyed on from the Negeb as far as Bethel, to the place where his tent had been at the beginning, between Bethel and Ai, to the place where he had made an altar at the first; and there Abram called on the name of the Lord." (13:3-4) In this matter also, the contrast is unmistakable: in both cases the protagonists in each story have experienced divine intervention on their behalf through plagues inflicted on Pharaoh (12:17). The ultimate irony in Joshua is that the people of "the ruin" were able to rout the Israelites as far as Shebarim, Hebrew for full destruction,[7] where they slew them (Josh 7:5a), the result of which was that "the hearts of the people melted, and became as water" (v.5b) and thus their fate ended up being similar to that of the nations around them (2:11; 5:1).

---

[7] The root *šabar* means "break" and *šebarim* is the plural of *šabar*.

Joshua's Prayer and God's Answer

At first hearing Joshua's prayer (7:6-9) sounds similar to
Moses' prayer after the people sinned in the wilderness (Ex
32:11-14). However, a more attentive ear will notice that, while
Moses appeals to God's own promise to the forefathers (v.13),
Joshua plays the card used in Ezekiel 20, that is, concern about
God's own name, which is tantamount to honor and fame in the
nations' eyes. Joshua's real interest, though, is his own "name"
and that of the people (Josh 7:9). Moreover, Joshua behaves like
Israel early on after the crossing of the Red Sea when they
blamed Moses for having led them out of Egypt into the
wilderness (Ex 14:11-12). Here Joshua is complaining that the
Lord made the people *cross* the Jordan when he should have left
them *across* it: "Alas, O Lord God, why hast thou *brought* this
people *over* the Jordan *at all* (*he'abarta ha'abir*; *made cross*
indeed), to give us into the hands of the Amorites, to destroy us?
Would that we had been content to dwell beyond (*be'eber*; *across*)
the Jordan!" (Josh 7:7) In other words, Joshua was complaining
about the "crossing" and blaming God for the ill-fated plan to
capture Ai, which did not succeed and thus the name of Israel
would not be glorified.

Joshua goes even so far as to repeat the stratagem he used
earlier: prostrating himself as a gesture of submission (7:10; see
5:14).[8] However, his scheme to blame the Lord and get his
people off the hook failed: "Israel has sinned; they have
transgressed (*'aberu*; crossed [over]) my covenant which I
commanded them; they have taken some of the devoted things;
they have stolen, and lied, and put them among their own stuff."
(7:11) Thus, the true mistake concerning the "crossing" has been

---

[8] In both cases we find virtually the same phrase "fall upon one's face" except for the
preposition: *naphal 'el panim* (5:14) and *naphal 'al panim* (7:10).

committed by Israel (see also v.15). Notice again the collective responsibility: although the actions that are condemned will be shown to be those of an individual, still it is all Israel that sinned. In breaking the divine *ḥerem* (anathema) they have become themselves under *ḥerem*, the object of anathema (v.12) and thus needed to be "sanctified" anew (v.13) as they had been earlier (3:5); otherwise, the Lord will cease to be "with you (*'immakem*)" (7:12).[9] The seriousness of the matter is underscored in v.15 where the transgression (crossing) of the covenant is further qualified as a "shameful thing" (*nebalah*) that needs to be exposed to the open, not hidden as Joshua was trying to do. The irony in the use here of *nebalah* on God's lips will be fully revealed in the following chapter where we encounter the only other occurrence of that noun in the book and no less than in conjunction with an action of extreme punishment taken by Joshua himself:

> So Joshua burned Ai, and made it for ever a heap of ruins, as it is to this day. And he hanged the king of Ai on a tree until evening; and at the going down of the sun Joshua commanded, and they took *his body* (*niblato*; his shamefulness) down from the tree, and cast it at the entrance of the gate of the city, and raised over it a great heap of stones, which stands there to this day. (8:28-29)

In Deuteronomy the action of exposing the body or carcass of an enemy leader by hanging it on a tree for all to see was intended to put the person to shame and thus to show him as "cursed": "And if a man has committed a crime punishable by death and he is put to death, and you hang him on a tree, his body (*niblato*; his shamefulness) shall not remain all night upon the tree, but you shall bury him the same day, for a hanged man is accursed

---

[9] This is the same term that is found in the good news statement "God is *with us*" (*'immanu 'el*) of Is 7:14.

by God." (21:22-23a) The irony lies in that Joshua followed the Law to a T when it came to the King of Ai and yet he tried to exonerate Israel of a similar *nebalah*. However, it is God who has the last word. Not only is the *nebalah* of the King of Ai remembered "to this day," but so also is Achan's and thus Israel's *nebalah* remembered and *in the same manner*: "And *they raised over him a great heap of stones* that remains to this day; then the Lord turned from his burning anger. Therefore *to this day* the name of that place is called the Valley of Achor." (7:26)

Before leaving this chapter it would be worthwhile to point out that, strangely enough, the first item that drew Achan's covetousness, even before the silver and gold, was "a beautiful mantle from Shinar" (v.21). The relevance of the reference to Shinar here is evident in that this is its only instance in the Prior Prophets, and that it occurs only eight times in the entire scriptural canon.[10] The first mention of "the land of Shinar" makes it clear that its location is in *'al 'iraq* (Iraq, Mesopotamia; Gen 10:10) where flourished the Assyrian empire, which destroyed Samaria (2 Kg 17), and the Babylonian empire, which subjugated Jerusalem (2 Kg 24:25). The hearer of the scriptural story, curious as to the value of the mention in Joshua that the mantle was from Shinar, will realize that Achan's disobedience, for which he and his immediate family were punished, as witnessed by "all Israel" (Josh 7:24), was only the first in a long series of similar actions that paved the way toward God's ultimate punishment of "all Israel." This, in turn, shows the importance of the introductory remark where Achan's infraction is introduced as the guilt of all "the children (people) of Israel" (v.1).

---

[10] The other instances, besides Josh 7:21, are Gen 10:10; 11:2; 14:1, 9; Is 11:11; Dan 1:2; Zech 5:11.

The Taking of Ai

Now that Israel is cleansed from the *ḥerem* and sanctified, God repeats his original command to Joshua "Do not fear or be dismayed" (8:1; see 1:9) and shows himself again as the strategist (8:2). In order to eliminate any overconfidence, which earlier cost the debacle before the inhabitants of Ai (7:5), Joshua takes along "*all* the fighting men," thirty thousand (8:3) instead of three thousand (7:4) in order to "seize" (*horaštem*; disinherit) the city (8:7). However, the city is not to become the people's own inheritance since it is slated, as Jericho before it, to be God's own property to deal with *as he pleases*, and the people are summoned to abide by "the Lord's word" issued for the occasion. Although Jericho was slated to full *ḥerem* (6:21), the divine bidding regarding Ai is more nuanced. Israel is not allowed to take any of the inhabitants of that city alive in order to enslave them into their personal property (8:8 and 24); the only booty they are allowed to take is "the cattle and the spoil of that city, *according to the word of the Lord which he commanded Joshua*" (v.27; see also v.2). The aim of such unexpected change is to remind the hearers that God does *as he pleases* with the earth that is and remains exclusively his.

The Reading of the Law

It is precisely at this point that the Law, containing all God's words of commandment, is read aloud to the hearing of "*all Israel*, sojourner as well as homeborn" (v.33) and "before all the assembly of Israel, and the women, and the little ones, and the sojourners who lived among them" (v.35). The rule of God, as King (*melek*) and thus proprietor of the earth of Canaan, applies to *all* of its residents. Even those who were circumcised (5:2-9) and celebrated Passover (vv.10-12) still transgressed God's will (ch.6) and needed to be chastised (ch.7). Being the children of Abraham through circumcision is not enough since the promise of the earth is contingent on the circumcision of the heart, that is to say, on abiding by the divine will as Abraham did:

> Now there was a famine in the land, besides the former famine that was in the days of Abraham. And Isaac went to Gerar, to Abimelech king of the Philistines. And the Lord appeared to him, and said, "Do not go down to Egypt; dwell in the land of which I shall tell you. Sojourn in this land, and I will be with you, and will bless you; for to you and to your descendants I will give all these lands, and I will fulfil the oath which I swore to Abraham your father. I will multiply your descendants as the stars of heaven, and will give to your descendants all these lands; and by your descendants all the nations of the earth shall bless themselves: *because Abraham obeyed my voice and kept my charge, my commandments, my statutes, and my laws.*" (Gen 26:1-5)

Now that his descendants are on that earth, the Law of Moses is reissued to them as an eternal reminder "that man does not live by bread alone, but that man (*ha'adam*; every human being) lives by everything that proceeds out of the mouth of the Lord" (Deut 8:3b).

10

Covenant of Peace with the Gibeonites

The story in chapter 9 takes us a step beyond that of Rahab. In the case of Rahab, Israel was bound through oath to return the favor, so to speak. Here one learns that Israel is to treat others well unconditionally just as and because the Lord did the same to it.

First we are told that Joshua and the leaders of Israel were lured into a covenant of peace with the Gibeonites (v.15). Further we learn that this covenant took place at "the camp at Gilgal" (v.6) where Israel had "camped" and kept the first Passover in Canaan (5:10). Passover is precisely the feast that commemorates the crossing of the Red Sea toward the holy mountain where God would make a covenant with the sinful and recalcitrant Israel. So the hearers are prepared to accept, or at least tolerate, another covenant although it was secured through human cunning (9:4). The intended parallelism between the two covenants is evident in the following features of the story:

1. The technical phrase "cut (*karat*; make) a covenant" to speak of the Mosaic covenant pervades the entire episode that seems to revolve around it (vv.6, 7, 11, 15, 16) and is only found once more in the book in conjunction with Joshua's instituting the Mosaic covenant with the people (24:25).

2. The seriousness of the covenant is reflected in that it was sworn to by the leaders of the congregation (*'edah*); *'edah* is the designation of Israel's official gathering in the Lord's presence

and which speaks in his name.[1] The sacredness of
such oath is underscored at the end of the story:
"But the people of Israel did not kill them [the
Gibeonites], because the leaders of the
congregation had sworn to them by the Lord, the
God of Israel. Then all the congregation
murmured against the leaders. But all the leaders
said to all the congregation, 'We have sworn to
them by the Lord, the God of Israel, and now we
may not touch them. This we will do to them,
and let them live, lest wrath (*qeṣeph*) be upon us,
because of the oath which we swore to them.'"
(vv.18-20) The gravity of the threat can be
gathered from the fact that the noun *qeṣeph*
occurs only once more in the book to speak of
the divine punishment inflicted on Achan and his
family: "Did not Achan the son of Zerah break
faith in the matter of the devoted things, and
wrath (*qeṣeph*) fell upon all the congregation of
Israel? And he did not perish alone for his
iniquity." (22:20)

3. Joshua's intervention in the Gibeonites' behalf is
   presented as "deliverance" using the same
   technical verb *hiṣṣil* that occurs repeatedly in
   Exodus 18 to qualify God's action of salvation
   toward Israel at the exodus (vv.4, 8, 9, 10).

4. Finally, although Joshua punishes the Gibeonites
   for their deception and condemns them to be
   slaves, still a careful hearing of the original

---

[1] See 18:1; 20:6, 9; 22:16-20, 30.

Hebrew will discern that the phraseology puts them in a similar situation as the Israelites at the exodus: they are kept alive in order to be "slaves/servants" (in the service) of the Lord (9:23, 24, 27). This word play is evident in the original, where both the Gibeonites and Moses are *'ebed*, but it is obscured in RSV that renders the same original *'ebed* into "slave" (v.23) and "servant" (v.24): "'Now therefore you are cursed, and some of you shall always be *slaves* (*'ebed*), hewers of wood and drawers of water for the house of my God.' They answered Joshua, 'Because it was told to *your servants* (*'abadeyka*) for a certainty that the Lord your God had commanded *his servant* (*'abdo*) Moses to give you all the land, and to destroy all the inhabitants of the land from before you; so we feared greatly for our lives because of you, and did this thing.'" (vv.23-24) Furthermore, since the status of the Gibeonites as "servants of the Lord" is for posterity, its effectiveness remains "to this day": "But Joshua made them that day hewers of wood and drawers of water for the congregation and *for the altar of the Lord, to continue to this day,* in the place which he should choose." (v.27) The enduring aspect of their being in the "service" of the Lord for posterity can be detected in the original phrasing of the "curse" (v.23). What is rendered in RSV as "some of you shall always be slaves" is actually "there shall not be cut off from among you a servant" (*lo' yikkaret mikkem 'ebed*), that is to say, "throughout your progeny there

shall always be found someone to serve" in the
"house of my God." A very clear case that
corroborates this understanding is found in
Jeremiah: "In those days Judah will be saved and
Jerusalem will dwell securely. And this is the
name by which it will be called: 'The Lord is our
righteousness.' For thus says the Lord: *David
shall never lack a man* (*lo' yikkaret ledawid 'iš*;
there shall not be cut off in David's lineage a
man) to sit on the throne of the house of Israel,
and *the Levitical priests shall never lack a man*
(*lakkohanim halewiyyim lo' yikkaret 'iš*;
throughout the lineage of the Levitical priests
there shall be cut off a man) in my presence to
offer burnt offerings, to burn cereal offerings, and
to make sacrifices for ever." (33:16-18) Still, in
the context of Joshua 9, there is yet another twist
that corroborates the positive aspect of *lo' yikkaret*
(there shall not be cut off): since a covenant
"with them [the Gibeonites], *to let them live*" was
"cut," none among them, though a slave, shall be
"cut (out)."

This last point can be termed as "merciful punishment": a life
sentence instead of a capital punishment, as was the case with
Adam's transgression. Both Genesis 3 and Joshua 9 are similar in
that the dispensed "curse" is the result of the intended "cunning"
on the part of the culprit. Not only is cunning as a noun
(*'ormah*) and as an adjective (*'arom* or *'arum*) extremely rare
outside the *ketubim*, the Wisdom literature of the Old

Testament,[2] but also the combination of cunning and curse is exclusive to Genesis 3 and Joshua 9. Such cannot be a coincidence. For the hearers, the lesson in mercy is to allow the perpetrator another chance to do well: if the serpent's cunning cost it, as well as Adam and Eve, a lesser sentence of curse than of death when no covenant was involved, then the Gibeonites are all the more entitled to such, especially that they are protected by a covenant taken under oath. In its way, this lesson doubles up with that heard in conjunction with Rahab, the harlot. However, the lesson of Joshua 9 is more pertinent given that the people had just heard "all the words of the law, the blessing and the curse,[3] according to all that is written in the book of the law" (8:34). At one point they heard that, after the sin of idolatry, tantamount to harlotry (Ex 34:15-16), committed by the Israelites while Moses was on the mountain (Ex 32), the Lord renewed the covenant (34:1-5a) giving them a second chance, proclaiming:

> The Lord, the Lord, a God merciful and gracious, slow to anger, and abounding in steadfast love and faithfulness, keeping steadfast love for thousands, forgiving iniquity and transgression and sin, but who will by no means clear the guilty, visiting the iniquity of the fathers upon the children and the children's children, to the third and the fourth generation. (vv.6b-7)

Israel need beware of breaking the covenant with Gibeonites in the future, especially that they have acquiesced to Joshua's verdict as "good (*tob*) and right (*yašar*; upright, correct, straight, straightforward)" (Josh 9:25). The Hebrew *yašar* has the

---

[2] *'ormah* occurs only in Ex 21:14 (*be'ormah*; treacherously) and Josh 9:4 (*be'ormah*; with cunning), *'arom* only in Gen 3:1 (subtle), and *'arum* only in 1 Sam 23:22 (cunning).

[3] The original Hebrew *qelalah* is from a completely different root than *'arur* (cursed [singular]; Gen 3:14) and *'arurim* (cursed [plural]; Josh 9:23).

connotation of being straight as a ruler, which is the carpenter's "rule" in Old English. In other words, one is *yašar* to the extent to which one is or behaves according to a given rule. Consequently, the author is saying that Joshua passed muster in following to a T the divine law according to the Lord's express summons to him (1:7) in his dealing with the Gibeonites, even "delivering them out of the hand of the people of Israel" (9:26). In so doing, he exonerated himself from his previous not so upright complaint when he tried to defend that same people and to blame God for their failure (7:6-9). Joshua's behavior toward the Gibeonites functions as test for his being *yašar*. Corroboration for this is found in the immediately following episode.

11

The Settlement

Coalition of the Amorite Kings and Settlement in the South

When a coalition of five kings planned to attack Gibeon, "for it has made peace with Joshua and with the people of Israel" (10:4), the Gibeonites asked Joshua for "help" (root *'azar*; v.4). The previous instance of "help" is found in 1:14 where the Trans-Jordan tribes were asked to help their brethren to settle in Canaan. The intended link is reflected in that, in both cases, the help is secured through *gibbore haḥayl* (men of valor [1:14]; mighty men of valor [10:7]). The message is clear: Gibeonites are entitled to the same kind of help as that given to Israelites. Further, this help is presented as "salvation" (root *yaša'*), whose meaning parallels that of "deliverance" (*hiṣṣil*) in that it also refers to the salvation wrought at the Red Sea: "Thus the Lord saved (*wayyoša'*) Israel that day from the hand of the Egyptians; and Israel saw the Egyptians dead upon the seashore." (Ex 14:30) What is interesting in this case is that salvation (*yešu'ah*) is still wrought by God, however at the hand of Joshua (*yehošu'a*):

And as they fled before Israel, while they were going down the ascent of Bethhoron, *the Lord threw down great stones* from heaven upon them as far as Azekah, and they died; there were more who died because of the hailstones than the men of Israel killed with the sword ... There has been no day like it before or since, when the Lord hearkened to the voice of a man; *for the Lord fought for Israel* ... [And Joshua said:] pursue your enemies, fall upon their rear, do not let them enter their cities; *for the Lord your God has given them into your hand* ... And Joshua took all these kings and their land at one time, *because the Lord God of Israel fought for Israel.* (Josh 10:11, 14, 19, 42)

Since victory was the Lord's work, all five cities were slated to the *ḥerem* in a detailed passage (vv.28-39) where the causative verb *heḥerim* (declare as *ḥerem* [anathema]) occurs five times, and is translated as "utterly destroyed" in the story (RSV vv.28, 35, 37, 39, 40).

The verdict of the Gibeonites that Joshua was *yašar* (9:25) is now validated by God himself who honored Joshua with a book bearing his name:

> Then spoke Joshua to the Lord in the day when the Lord gave the Amorites over to the men of Israel; and he said in the sight of Israel, "Sun, stand thou still at Gibeon, and thou Moon in the valley of Aijalon." And the sun stood still, and the moon stayed, until the nation took vengeance on their enemies. Is this not written in the Book of Jashar (*hayyašar*: the upright one)? The sun stayed in the midst of heaven, and did not hasten to go down for about a whole day. There has been no day like it before or since, when the Lord hearkened to the voice of a man; for the Lord fought for Israel. (10:12-14)

Imagining an extra-canonical "Book of Jashar" that was lost, as scholarship has surmised, is as improbable as the premise of the equally "lost" Q document that allegedly contained the "Sayings of Jesus." The "Book of the Upright One" is none other than the Book of Joshua that contains the standing still of both the sun and the moon and "there has been no day like it before *or since*," that is to say, a day unique in history, unrepeated and unrepeatable, just as the "Mosaic" Book of Exodus contains the sole account of the crossing of the Red Sea, an event that is as well unrepeated and unrepeatable, which explains why it can only be remembered. It is only by listening to the Book of Joshua that one learns that the sun stood still at Gibeon to allow complete victory before it set!

The Coalition of Kings and the Settlement in the North

After taking the main cities in south Canaan, from Kadeshbarnea to Gibeon (10:41), Joshua turns his attention to the north. The story follows the same pattern as the previous one: the opponent is a coalition of kings (11:1-4) that are defeated at "the waters of Merom" (vv.5, 7), just as the previous coalition was routed at Gibeon (10:10). Similarly, the rule of the *ḥerem* is applied (11:11, 12, 20, 21). Since the coverage of the "battles" ends at the close of this chapter (v.23b) the last two passages are summative:

1. The first passage (vv.15-20) is a reminder that all Joshua "did" was to execute that which the Lord commanded Moses, his servant, which forms an *inclusio* with the start of the book (1:1, 6-9). Just as Joshua's "crossing" of the Jordan is patterned after Moses' "crossing of the Red Sea," so also Joshua's victory is an echo of that of Moses. In both cases victory came through direct intervention by God himself: the hardening of Pharaoh's heart (Ex 4:21; 7:3; 9:12; 10:1, 20, 27; 11:10; 14:4, 8, 17), and the hardening of the heart of the inhabitants of Canaan (Josh 11:20). Still, against this background of total victory, one hears a final reminder of the thorny issue of Gibeon (11:19): salvation and redemption will always remain under God's conditions.

2. The second passage (vv.21-23b) concludes with a reference to the tribal allotments *as heritage*: "So Joshua took the whole land (earth), according to all that the Lord had spoken to Moses; and Joshua gave it for an inheritance (*naḥalah*) to Israel according to their tribal allotments (*maḥleqot*; from the same root as *ḥeleq*)." To stress this point—that the earth is a gift from God—the previous two verses refer to the Anakim of whom the people were initially afraid, which fear induced them to rebel against the Lord (Deut 1:26-28). Yet the Lord assured them with these words:

> Hear, O Israel; you are to pass over the Jordan this day, to go in to dispossess nations greater and mightier than yourselves, cities great and fortified up to heaven, a people great and tall, the sons of the Anakim, whom you know, and of whom you have heard it said, 'Who can stand before the sons of Anak?" Know therefore this day that *he who goes over* ('*ober*; *crosses over*) *before you as a devouring fire is the Lord your God*; *he will destroy them and subdue them before you*; so you shall drive them out (*horaštam*; disinherit them), and make them perish quickly, as the Lord has promised you. (9:1-3)

Thus, both of these passages are sub-tunes of the same tune: "the Lord is the "master" (*'adon*) of all the earth", a statement heard twice (Josh 3:11, 13), for underscoring, just before the crossing into Canaan (vv.14-17).

Since chapters 10 and 11 referred to coalitions of kings, before going into detailing the tribal allotments (chs. 13-21) the author goes over the list of kings whose cities were overtaken (ch. 12). Chapter 12 is clearly linked to the previous chapter in that it takes up the idea of heritage underscored in 11:23. "Now these are the kings of the land (earth), whom the people of Israel defeated, and took possession of (*yirešu*; inherited) their land (earth)." (12:1) Moreover, as was the case in 11:15-20, Joshua's work (12:7-24) is referred to as a continuation of that of his predecessor Moses (vv.1-6). Notice how the last verse, which makes mention of Moses, is cast in the same vocabulary as v.1: "Moses, the servant of the Lord, and the people of Israel *defeated* them; and Moses the servant of the Lord gave their land for a possession (*yeruššah*; inheritance, heritage) to the Reubenites and the Gadites and the half-tribe of Manasseh." (v.6)

Looking ahead to the rest of the story covered in the Prior Prophets, the author begins the detailed account of the allotment yet reminds the hearers that the promise of inheritance will not be fulfilled during Joshua's lifetime (13:1-7). Still that should not be a matter of worry, since as it has been up until then, the Lord himself will ensure the future success of his plan, and that is why Joshua should finish the duty of allotment assigned to him: "I will myself drive them out (*'orišem*; disinherit them) from before the people of Israel; only allot the land to Israel for an inheritance (*nahalah*), as I have commanded you. Now therefore divide (*halleq*; allot) this land for an inheritance (*nahalah*) to the nine tribes and half the tribe of Manasseh." (vv.6b-7) To ensure that the readers will trust this statement, the author reminds them that the Trans-Jordan allotments were actually implemented by Moses, before Joshua took over the mantle of leadership (vv.8-33).

At the end of the introductory section to this passage (vv.8-13) the hearer is reminded twice of the fact underscored earlier, namely, that the Lord remains the proprietor (*melek*; king) and master (*'adon*) of *all the earth* with which he does *as he pleases*. On the one hand, "the people of Israel did not drive out (*horišu*; disinherit) the Geshurites or the Maacathites; but Geshur and Maacath *dwell in the midst of Israel to this day.*" (v.13) On the other hand, "To the tribe of Levi alone Moses gave no inheritance (*naḥalah*); the offerings by fire to the Lord God of Israel are their inheritance (*naḥalah*), as he said to him." (v.14) The importance of this statement is evident in the fact that it is repeated at the end of section (v.33). The matter of that tribe's inheritance will be dealt with specifically and in detail in chapter 21.

12

Caleb

The introductory passage to the allotments of the nine and a half remaining tribes (14:1-5) reiterates that Joshua's work is a continuation of the one God started with Moses. It also reminds the hearer of the special status accorded the tribe of Levi (vv.3-4). What is striking, however, is that, before discussing the tribes one by one, starting with Judah (ch.15), the author begins by treating the case of Caleb independently (14:6-15), although he is still an integral part of the Judah tribe (15:13-19). So why Caleb?

The immediate straightforward answer to this question lies in the episode of Numbers 13-14 to which Caleb makes reference here and which, chronologically, precedes the trek through Trans-Jordan (Num 20-25; 32-34) at the end of which we hear:

> The Lord said to Moses, "These are the names of the men who shall divide the land to you for inheritance: Eleazar the priest and Joshua the son of Nun. You shall take one leader of every tribe, to divide the land for inheritance. These are the names of the men: Of the tribe of Judah, Caleb the son of Jephunneh ..." (34:16-19)

However, the scriptural story of Caleb has much more to offer than most modern hearers can discern if they do not know the meaning of names in the original languages and, consequently, consider the named locations, as well as individuals, a series of "what-shall-I-call-it or him or her."[1] This is especially true in the

---

contemporary United States where the almost sacred importance given personal names is aimed at underscoring individuality rather than commonality. Although Joshua appears for the first time early on during the wandering in the wilderness (Ex 17:9), the first mention of Caleb is relegated to Numbers 13:6. This sequence is clearly functional: Joshua was present at the promulgation of the Law (Ex 20-24) while Caleb was not. One can then surmise that Caleb was a Gentile, a member of the "nations." Both his name and his affiliation militate for such. The Hebrew consonantal trilateral *klb* means "dog" (*keleb*), which is used pejoratively for an outsider, an impure and thus worthless entity, as is clear from the following scriptural instances:

You shall be men consecrated to me; therefore you shall not eat any flesh that is torn by beasts in the field; you shall cast it to the dogs (*keleb*; dog). (Ex 22:31)

You shall not bring the hire of a harlot, or the wages of a dog (*keleb*), into the house of the Lord your God in payment for any vow; for both of these are an abomination to the Lord your God. (Deut 23:18)

And the Philistine said to David, "Am I a dog (*keleb*), that you come to me with sticks?" And the Philistine cursed David by his gods. (1 Sam 17:43)

After whom has the king of Israel come out? After whom do you pursue? After a dead dog (*keleb*)! After a flea! (1 Sam 24:14)

Then Abner was very angry over the words of Ishbosheth, and said, "Am I a dog's (*keleb*) head of Judah? This day I keep showing

---

Zacchaeus, as publican, was considered impure by the Pharisees, his actions of mercy "atoned" him and thus Jesus could declare him a "son of Abraham" with whom he could share table fellowship.

loyalty to the house of Saul your father, to his brothers, and to his friends, and have not given you into the hand of David; and yet you charge me today with a fault concerning a woman." (2 Sam 3:8)

And he did obeisance, and said, "What is your servant, that you should look upon a dead dog (*keleb*) such as I?" (2 Sam 9:8)

Then Abishai the son of Zeruiah said to the king, "Why should this dead dog (*keleb*) curse my lord the king? Let me go over and take off his head." (2 Sam 16:9)

And Hazael said, "What is your servant, who is but a dog (*keleb*), that he should do this great thing?" Elisha answered, "The Lord has shown me that you are to be king over Syria." (2 Kg 8:13)

He who slaughters an ox is like him who kills a man; he who sacrifices a lamb, like him who breaks a dog's (*keleb*) neck; he who presents a cereal offering, like him who offers swine's blood; he who makes a memorial offering of frankincense, like him who blesses an idol. These have chosen their own ways, and their soul delights in their abominations. (Is 66:3)

Further, Caleb is a Kenizzite (Num 32:12; Josh 14:6, 14). The only other occurrence of Kenizzite in scripture occurs in a passage where the inhabitants of the earth of the promise are listed as ten nations: "On that day the Lord made a covenant with Abram, saying, 'To your descendants I give this land (earth), from the river of Egypt to the great river, the river Euphrates, the land (earth) of the Kenites, the Kenizzites, the Kadmonites, the Hittites, the Perizzites, the Rephaim, the Amorites, the Canaanites, the Girgashites and the Jebusites.'" (Gen 15:18-21) The closeness to the other three instances in the original Hebrew is evident in that in the list of nations each nation is mentioned in the generic singular; thus the original for "the Kenizzites" is *haqqenizzi* (the Kenizzite), which is precisely the surname of Caleb in Numbers and Joshua. Can then one surmise that the Kenizzite in Genesis is intentionally introduced with an eye toward Caleb? The answer should be in the affirmative since the context is the promise of the inheritance and, furthermore, we hear of "until the great river, the river Euphrates," a phrase that occurs only twice more (Deut 1:7; Josh 1:4) again in relation to that same promise. On the other hand, since the numeral ten is reflective of totality, those ten nations (Gen 15:18-21) represent "all the nations" and, consequently, any one of them is representative of all of them. Given all of the above, one can conclude that Caleb the Kenizzite is tantamount to Caleb the "Gentile," as a counterpart to Joshua the Israelite.

This reading is further corroborated in that the choice of the numeral ten is clearly intended, and not happenstance. When one notices that the longest lists of nations residing in the earth of promise comprise seven names, then the choice of three more—the Kenites, the Kenizzites, the Kadmonites—becomes quite striking, especially that the additional three names are at the beginning of the list and are extremely rare in scripture. A closer look at these names will result in further support for this thesis. The Kenite (*qeyni*; Cainite) is a descendant of Cain (*qayn*) as is evident from the following statement: "Now Heber the Kenite (*qeyni*; Cainite) had separated (derives) from Cain (*qayn*),[2] the descendants of Hobab the father-in-law of Moses, and had pitched his tent as far away as the oak in Zaanannim,

---

[2] RSV has "the Kenites." Although JB is closer to the original (Heber the Kenite had parted company with the tribe of Kain), still it is misleading in that (1) it changes its usual "Cain" into "Kain" and (2) supplies "the tribe of" before Kain, which is not in the original Hebrew.

which is near Kedesh." (Judg 4:11)[3] Cain is the first human born outside the garden of Eden and thus the father of all humans and, as such, the archetypal representative of the nations. The Kadmonite (*qadmoni*) means the Easterner, from *qedem* (east) where precisely Cain settled after his father Adam: "He [the Lord God] drove out the man; and *at the east* (*miqqedem*) of the garden of Eden" (Gen 3:24a); "Then Cain went away from the presence of the Lord, and dwelt in the land of Nod, *east of* (*qidmat*) Eden." (4:16) Considering that *qedem* means also "before," the only other two scriptural occurrences of *qadmoni* confirm the technical meaning of that adjectival noun: "As the proverb of *the ancients* (*haqqadmoni*; the ancient one) says, 'Out of the wicked comes forth wickedness'; but my hand shall not be against you" (1 Sam 24:13); "I will remove the northerner far from you, and drive him into a parched and desolate land, his front into the eastern (*haqqadmoni*) sea, and his rear into the western sea." (Joel 2:20) So, if the first and third name in the cluster point in the same direction, namely, to the human being in general as an individual member of any nation, then it stands to reason to consider the central adjective as functioning similarly. The patient hearer will be later rewarded to learn that the quintessential representative of the "nations" is Caleb, *the* Kenizzite. How about Jephunneh, Caleb's father? The Hebrew

---

[3] In this regard it would be worth noting that, earlier in Judges, we actually hear of a "direct" connection between Caleb as Judahite (Josh 14:1) and the Kenites. In Judg 1:9-15 the tribe of Judah takes Hebron, Caleb's heritage (v.10), and then Caleb is personally involved in the taking of Debir (vv.11-15) during which episode we learn that his daughter Achsah resides in the Negeb area (v.15). Immediately thereafter, the mention of the Negeb triggers the following appendix: "And the descendants of the Kenite, Moses' father-in-law, went up *with the people of Judah* from the city of palms into the wilderness of Judah, which lies in the Negeb near Arad; and *they went and settled with the people*." (v.16)

yephunneh means "he clears up, opens up" and thus "prepares."[4] This action fits perfectly Caleb and his mission: to prepare the way for the inheritance of Canaan and to be the first to be mentioned as having secured his allotment (Josh 14:6-15) in Canaan proper (v.1).

We are told repeatedly that Caleb's place of honor was granted to him because he "wholly followed the Lord" (Num 32:11-12; Deut 1:36; Josh 14:8, 9, 14), although he was not privy to the promulgation of the Law! It is worth noting the crescendo in Joshua 14. First we hear the confession on Caleb's lips: "I wholly followed the Lord *my God.*" (v.8) Then it is Moses who recognizes that Caleb wholly followed the Lord, *Moses' God*: "And Moses swore on that day, saying, 'Surely the land on which your foot has trodden shall be an inheritance for you and your children for ever, because you have wholly followed the Lord *my God.*'" (v.9) Finally, the author puts his seal on the matter: "So Hebron became the inheritance of Caleb the son of Jephunneh the Kenizzite to this day, because he wholly followed the Lord, *the God of Israel.*" (v.14) The faithfulness of Caleb, the Gentile, to God's law was rewarded with his having been granted Hebron, the choicest piece of the heritage (v.13). The importance, if not outright centrality, of this city can be gathered from a quick glance at its "story." Not only is it Abram's first dwelling in Canaan (Gen 13:18) immediately after the divine promise that he would inherit the surrounding earth "as far as he can see" (vv.14-17), but it is also the place where the forefathers and foremothers of the scriptural Israel sojourned (35:27; 37:14) and were buried (23:2, 19; 35:29; 49:31; 50:1-14). Thus

---

[4] See the eight scriptural occurrences: Gen 24:31; Lev 14:36; Is 40:3; 57:14; 62:10; Zeph 3:15 (has cast out [has cleared away]); Mal 3:1; Ps 80:9.

Hebron, as its Hebrew name *ḥebron* indicates, is the communal place of gathering, the place of encompassing brotherhood.[5]

Co-inheritance with the Nations

Looking back at the itinerary of the entrance into Canaan that culminates with its inheritance (Josh 14), one detects a sub-theme of the book, which is the corollary of its main theme that the Lord is the lord (master) of all the earth (3:11, 13). The sub-theme is that this same Lord's plan as well as his initial decision is the co-inheritance of his earth by Israel and the nations. The story encompassing both the preparation for and the actual crossing into Canaan is bracketed with the case of Rahab, the Canaanite harlot (2:1 and 6:25). At the heart of this lengthy episode we have the passage about the "covenant" of circumcision, which in turn brings to mind Genesis 17 where Abraham is specifically introduced as "the father of a multitude of nations" (v.4) and, on such basis, circumcision is intended as encompassing "both he that is born in your house and he that is bought with your money from any foreigner who is not of your offspring" (vv.12-13). That is why "she [Rahab] dwelt in (the midst of; *beqereb*) Israel *to this day*" (Josh 6:25b).

However, since the "crossing" into Canaan was marred by the people's disobedience in spite of their being circumcised, the second part of the book, which deals with the beginning of the "settlement" in Canaan (chs.7-12), revolves around the proclamation of the Law (8:30-35). In this regard, Israel's obedience to the "covenant" of the Law had to be tested as to whether they would keep a "covenant" of peace with the inhabitants of Gibeon (ch.9) who were Hivites (11:19). The

---

[5] The Hebrew *ḥeber* means "company, community" and the Hebrew *ḥaber* means "companion, member of a community."

centrality of this test for the story is evident in that the "need" of the Gibeonites triggered the first period in the "settlement" (10:1-9) that ended with chapter 12. This "covenant" with the Gentile Hivites will haunt Israel and its kings throughout the centuries (2 Sam 21:1-14).

The last indication of the sub-theme of co-inheritance with the nations is after the interlude of chapter 13 covering the heritage of the Trans-Jordan tribes. The author heads the final stage of the settlement in Canaan by the nine and half tribes with a special section on the "Gentile" Caleb. Thus when listening to the settlement of the Israelite tribes, the hearer will realize that these are co-inheriting that earth with the nations. A series of passages corroborate that God's will for Canaan is that it be a prototype for all parts of God's earth—an earth intended for co-habitation for all children of Adam:

Yet the people of Israel did not drive out the Geshurites or the Maacathites; but Geshur and Maacath dwell in the midst of Israel *to this day.* (Josh 13:13)

But the Jebusites, the inhabitants of Jerusalem, the people of Judah could not drive out; so the Jebusites dwell with the people of Judah at Jerusalem *to this day.* (15:63)

However they [the Ephraimites] did not drive out the Canaanites that dwelt in Gezer: so the Canaanites have dwelt in the midst of Ephraim *to this day.* (16:10)

But the people of Benjamin did not drive out the Jebusites who dwelt in Jerusalem; so the Jebusites have dwelt with the people of Benjamin in Jerusalem *to this day.* (Judg 1:21)[6]

---

[6] An indication that Caleb was originally an outsider can be seen in the phraseology concerning his inheritance: "According to the commandment of the Lord to Joshua,

Manasseh did not drive out the inhabitants of Bethshean and its villages, or Taanach and its villages, or the inhabitants of Dor and its villages, or the inhabitants of Ibleam and its villages, or the inhabitants of Megiddo and its villages; but the Canaanites persisted in dwelling in that earth. When Israel grew strong, they put the Canaanites to forced labor, but did not utterly drive them out. And Ephraim did not drive out the Canaanites who dwelt in Gezer; but the Canaanites dwelt in Gezer among them. Zebulun did not drive out the inhabitants of Kitron, or the inhabitants of Nahalol; but the Canaanites dwelt among them, and became subject to forced labor. (Judg 1:27:30)

Furthermore, just as other populations dwell in the midst of or with the children of Israel, so the converse is true:

Asher did not drive out the inhabitants of Acco, or the inhabitants of Sidon, or of Ahlab, or of Achzib, or of Helbah, or of Aphik, or of Rehob; but *the Asherites dwelt among the Canaanites, the inhabitants of the earth*; for they did not drive them out. *Naphtali* did not drive out the inhabitants of Bethshemesh, or the inhabitants of Beth-anath, but *dwelt among the Canaanites, the inhabitants of the earth*; nevertheless the inhabitants of Bethshemesh and of Beth-anath became subject to forced labor for them. (Judg 1:27-33)

---

he gave to Caleb the son of Jephunneh a portion (*ḥeleq*; lot) *among the people (children) of Judah*, Kiriatharba, that is, Hebron (Arba was the father of Anak)." (Josh 15:13)

13

The Allotment to the Tribes

Joshua 15 through 19 details the allotment of the heritages to the Cis-Jordan nine and a half tribes: Judah (ch.15), Ephraim (ch.16), the half tribe of Manasseh (ch.17), Benjamin (ch.18), Simeon, Zebulun, Issachar, Asher, Naphtali, and Dan (ch.19). The tribe of Levi had a special status and will be dealt with in chapters 20-21. In order to preserve the symbolic total number of twelve, the tribe of Joseph was split between his two children, Ephraim and Manasseh:

> And Jacob said to Joseph, "God Almighty appeared to me at Luz in the land of Canaan and blessed me, and said to me, 'Behold, I will make you fruitful, and multiply you, and I will make of you a company of peoples, and will give this land to your descendants after you for an everlasting possession.' And now your two sons, who were born to you in the land of Egypt before I came to you in Egypt, are mine; Ephraim and Manasseh shall be mine, as Reuben and Simeon are. And the offspring born to you after them shall be yours; they shall be called by the name of their brothers in their inheritance." (Gen 48:3-6)

In the census at the end of Numbers, the "sons of Joseph" (26:28) are divided into the "sons of Manasseh" (v.29) and the "sons of Ephraim" (v.35) while the members of the tribe of Levi are not introduced as "sons of" like the rest of the tribes,[1] but simply as "the Levites as numbered according to their families"

---

[1] Vv.5, 12, 15, 19, 23, 26, 28, 38, 42, 44, 48; see also vv.29 and 35.

(v.57). "Levite" refers to the priestly function rather than the progeny of Levi.[2]

The author starts with Judah because it is the tribe of Caleb and eventually King David. This primacy will be underscored clearly at the beginning of Judges: "After the death of Joshua the people of Israel inquired of the Lord, 'Who shall go up first (*battehillah*; at the beginning, at first) for us against the Canaanites, to fight against them?' The Lord said, 'Judah shall go up; behold, I have given the land into his hand.'" (1:1-2) The same primacy will also be upheld throughout the period of the Judges since, later in the war launched by all the other tribes against that of Benjamin, we are told: "The people of Israel arose and went up to Bethel, and inquired of God, 'Which of us shall go up first (*battehillah*) to battle against the Benjaminites?' And the Lord said, 'Judah shall go up first (*battehillah*).'" (Judg 20:18) One can sense that Caleb and David are on the author's mind. In spite of his having been allocated a long passage in the previous chapter, Caleb's case is revisited (Josh 15:13-19) beginning with his inheritance of Hebron (v.13). As for David, he is obliquely present through the reference to the Jebusites: "But the Jebusites, the inhabitants of Jerusalem, the people of Judah could not drive out; so the Jebusites dwell with the people of Judah at Jerusalem to this day." (v.63) Their city will be taken over by David while he was king at Hebron:

> So all the elders of Israel came to the king at Hebron; and King David made a covenant with them at Hebron before the Lord, and they anointed David king over Israel. David was thirty years old when he began to reign, and he reigned forty years. At Hebron

---

[2] Actually the Hebrew reads *pequde hallewi* (the numbered [ones] of *the* Levi[te]), with the definite article "the" before the name Levi.

he reigned over Judah seven years and six months; and at Jerusalem he reigned over all Israel and Judah thirty-three years. And the king and his men went to Jerusalem against the Jebusites, the inhabitants of the land, who said to David, "You will not come in here, but the blind and the lame will ward you off"—thinking, "David cannot come in here." Nevertheless David took the stronghold of Zion, that is, the city of David. (2 Sam 5:3-6)

Joshua 16 deals with the inheritance of Ephraim and chapter 17 with that of the other half tribe of Manasseh. The allotment of the heritages of the remaining seven tribes covers chapters 18 and 19. It is introduced with a passage centered round Shiloh, its first reference in scripture (18:1-10):[3]

> Then the whole congregation of the people of Israel assembled at Shiloh, and set up the tent of meeting there; the land lay subdued before them. There remained among the people of Israel seven tribes whose inheritance (*nahalah*) had not yet been apportioned (*halequ*) … Joshua cast lots for them in Shiloh before the Lord; and there Joshua apportioned (*yehalleq*) the land to the people of Israel, to each his portion (*mahleqah*). (vv.1-2, 10)

The special mention of the Levites in v.7a (The Levites have no portion among you, for the priesthood of the Lord is their heritage) prepares for the beginning of chapter 21 which contains the last episode of the allotment process: "Then the heads of the fathers' houses of the Levites came to Eleazar the priest and to Joshua the son of Nun and to the heads of the fathers' houses of the tribes of the people of Israel; and they said to them at Shiloh in the land of Canaan, 'The Lord commanded through Moses that we be given cities to dwell in, along with

---

[3] I am excepting Josh 16:6 where we find a reference to a locality named Taanathshiloh (*ta'anat siloh*) whose meaning in Hebrew is "the fig tree of Shiloh."

their pasture lands for our cattle.'" (vv.1-2) Similarly, the reference to the Trans-Jordan two and a half tribes (18:7b) looks ahead to the last mention of Shiloh in the book (22:9, 12) in conjunction with the misunderstanding between those tribes and their Cis-Jordan brethren concerning the building of another altar to the Lord in Trans-Jordan. Furthermore, the allotment takes place through casting of lots (18:10) "before the Lord, at the door of the tent of meeting" (19:51) to ensure that the hearers understand that the allotment of the heritages of the "lesser" tribes is as much willed by God as that of the major tribes of Judah, Ephraim, and Manasseh. Finally, the inclusion of the special heritage of Joshua (vv.49-50) is made here to justify the place of his burial referred to later in scripture (24:30; see also Judg 2:9).

14

The Cities of Refuge

Another function of the reference to Shiloh in the previous two chapters is to prepare for the necessity of establishing the cities of refuge (ch.22). As we shall learn in 1 Samuel, Shiloh will eventually become the first religious center for Israel: "Now this man [Elkanah][1] used to go up year by year from his city to worship and to sacrifice to the Lord of hosts at Shiloh, where the two sons of Eli, Hophni and Phinehas, were priests of the Lord." (1:3) At the demise of Eli (4:18a) for the sins of his two sons (3:11-12) we are told that "he had judged Israel forty years" (4:18b). Shiloh was abandoned (Jer 7:12-14; 26:6-9) and "Samuel," who took Eli's place, "judged the people of Israel at Mizpah" (1 Sam 7:6b). It is worthwhile, at this juncture, to point out another example of how scripture is more impressive, if not more meaningful, when it is heard in the original language. The Hebrew *mispah* (Mizpah) means "watchtower" and derives from *sippeh* (watch, look out) which occurs in the Prior Prophets only at 1 Samuel 4:13a, that is to say, a few verses before the demise of Eli, and in the following context:

> And the ark of God was captured; and the two sons of Eli, Hophni and Phinehas, were slain. A man of Benjamin ran from the battle line, and came to Shiloh the same day, with his clothes rent and with earth upon his head. When he arrived, Eli was sitting upon his seat by the road watching (*mesappeh*), for his heart trembled for the ark of God. And when the man came into the city and told the news, all the city cried out. (vv.11-13)

---

[1] Hannah's husband and father of Samuel.

Thus, the ark of the covenant was captured from Shiloh by the Philistines as punishment for the sin of Eli's sons. Eli was "watching" the seat of divine judgment being moved away from Shiloh to its new seat at Mizpah, the new "lookout" center for all Israel.

The most essential facet of the deity and its monarch is that of "judge." Without this, its "world" collapses.[2] In the absence of kingship, which is first relegated to Saul (1 Sam 8-12),[3] it is God himself who judges "all Israel" through Eli and then Samuel. However, before then, while the ark of the covenant had no permanent residence, that function of judging was implemented through the medium of the cities of refuge. These cities were established to protect the non-willful perpetrator of a homicide (Josh 20:1-5), Israelite and outsider alike (v.9). It is in those cities that that person would be judged by the assembled congregation ('edah; vv.6a, 9). The chance to establish the guilt was extended until the death of the high priest, head of the congregation. If the guilt of the perpetrator was not verified before the death of the high priest, then the perpetrator was free to return to his home (v.6b). This rule was established to protect the individuals against indiscriminate vengeance (v.5). The importance of that matter is reflected in that the cities of refuge were divided equally between the Cis-Jordan and Trans-Jordan territories (vv.7-8). The institution of the cities of refuge was ordained by God himself through Moses (v.2; see Num 35:9-34; Deut 19:1-13).

Joshua 21 deals with the heritage of the Levites. Although they were not given territories, they inherited "forty eight cities with

---

[2] For the deity, see Ps 82:1-8; 96:10, 13; 98:9; for the monarch, see Ps 45:6-7; 72:1-8, 12-16.
[3] With the exception of the aborted effort at such by Abimelech (Judg 9).

their pasture lands" interspersed throughout the domains of the twelve tribes (vv.41-42). Among the Levitical cities are six cities of refuge mentioned in 20:7-8: Hebron (21:13), Shechem (v.21), Golan (v.27), Kedesh (v.32), Bezer (v.36), and Ramoth (v.38). This was done in accordance with the instruction given in Numbers 35: "The cities which you give to the Levites shall be the six cities of refuge, where you shall permit the manslayer to flee, and in addition to them you shall give forty-two cities. All the cities which you give to the Levites shall be forty-eight, with their pasture lands." (vv.6-7)

The conclusion of chapter 21 is a summation of the Book of Joshua formally as well as materially in that it includes the book's basic terminology:

> Thus the Lord *gave* to Israel all the land (earth) which he *swore* to give to *their fathers*; and having taken possession of (*yirašu*; inherited) it, they settled (*yešebu*; dwelt) there. And the Lord *gave* them *rest* (*yanaḥ*) on every side just as he had *sworn* to their *fathers*; not one of all their enemies had withstood them, for the Lord had given all their enemies into their hands. Not *one* (*dabar*; item, matter) of all the good *promises* (*dabar*) which the Lord had made (*dibber*) to the house of Israel had failed; all came to pass. (Josh 21:43-45)

The concluding verse in the Hebrew is impressive in that the listener hears three times the same root *dabar* that is usually translated as "word" especially in the phrase *debar yahweh* (the word of the Lord). All that happened in the Book of Joshua is the result of the divine "word" and thus the contents of that book are ultimately a teaching, a lesson, a parabole rather than a factual report. The divine "plan" (Hebrew *dabar*; Greek *oikonomia*) is embedded in the "words" of scripture. The scriptural God and his "word" do not stand outside scripture;

rather they are "contained" within the scriptural "words." Put otherwise, God "comes" into our minds and hearts *out of* the actual words consigned in scripture. It is only *in them* that time and again he both *is* and *meets us* until he ultimately "comes" to judge us as to whether or not we have hearkened to *his words*.

15

The Altar in Trans-Jordan

Now that all the tribes are settled, the two and a half Trans-Jordan tribes can go to their own heritage (22:4a) where they had left "their wives, their little ones, and their cattle" (1:14). The author takes this occasion to underscore in the minds of the hearers the importance of the "one altar" that secures the oneness of the ark of covenant and thus of God himself (22:16-20). There was concern about the altar built by the Trans-Jordan tribes; however, they explained that the altar they built was only "formal" and not "functional." It will serve as a "witness" to the following generations on both sides of the Jordan that the Trans-Jordan tribes are no less part of Israel than the other ten tribes (vv.26-29). Although we are told that "the Reubenites, the Gadites, and the half-tribe of Manasseh said in answer to the heads of the families of Israel" (v.21), de facto it is more specifically only "the Reubenites and Gadites" (v.25) that are in a bind since half of the Manasseh tribe resides in Canaan proper. The problem raised by the duality of altars or temples will be exacerbated later under Jeroboam of Israel (1 Kg 12:26-13:34).

Joshua 23 functions as a hinge between the Books of Joshua and Judges. Although we are again reminded that God fulfilled his "word" of promise (v.14), still the "words" of his law encompass not only the blessing, but also the curse (8:34) that will become functional if the law is not upheld. That is why the aging Joshua begins by requiring of the people what the Lord required of him: "Therefore be very steadfast to keep and do all that is written in the book of the law of Moses, turning aside

from it neither to the right hand nor to the left." (23:6) Then he
ends his speech with the following warning:

> But just as all the good things which the Lord your God promised
> concerning you have been fulfilled for you, so the Lord will bring
> upon you all the evil things, until he have destroyed you from off
> this good land ('*adamah*; ground) which the Lord your God has
> given you, if you transgress the covenant of the Lord your God,
> which he commanded you, and go and serve other gods and bow
> down to them. Then the anger of the Lord will be kindled against
> you, and you shall perish quickly from off the good land ('*ereṣ*;
> earth) which he has given to you. (vv. 15-16)

It is precisely this menace that will form the crimson thread
throughout the Book of Judges:

> And the people of Israel did what was evil in the sight of the Lord
> and served the Baals; and they forsook the Lord, the God of their
> fathers, who had brought them out of the land of Egypt; they
> went after other gods, from among the gods of the peoples who
> were round about them, and bowed down to them; and they
> provoked the Lord to anger. They forsook the Lord, and served
> the Baals and the Ashtaroth. So the anger of the Lord was kindled
> against Israel, and he gave them over to plunderers, who
> plundered them; and he sold them into the power of their enemies
> round about, so that they could no longer withstand their
> enemies. Whenever they marched out, the hand of the Lord was
> against them for evil, as the Lord had warned, and as the Lord had
> sworn to them; and they were in sore straits. Then the Lord raised
> up judges, who saved them out of the power of those who
> plundered them. And yet they did not listen to their judges; for
> they played the harlot after other gods and bowed down to them;
> they soon turned aside from the way in which their fathers had
> walked, who had obeyed the commandments of the Lord, and
> they did not do so. Whenever the Lord raised up judges for them,
> the Lord was with the judge, and he saved them from the hand of

their enemies all the days of the judge; for the Lord was moved to pity by their groaning because of those who afflicted and oppressed them. But whenever the judge died, they turned back and behaved worse than their fathers, going after other gods, serving them and bowing down to them; they did not drop any of their practices or their stubborn ways. So the anger of the Lord was kindled against Israel; and he said, "Because this people have transgressed my covenant which I commanded their fathers, and have not obeyed my voice, I will not henceforth drive out before them any of the nations that Joshua left when he died, that by them I may test Israel, whether they will take care to walk in the way of the Lord as their fathers did, or not." So the Lord left those nations, not driving them out at once, and he did not give them into the power of Joshua. (Judg 2:11-23)

16

The Renewal of the Mosaic Covenant

Joshua 24 is arguably one of the most central chapters in scripture. It sums up the message of the book and, at the same time, sets the stage for the story relayed in the Prior Prophets. Its main feature is the renewal of the Mosaic covenant with a new generation that neither left Egypt nor wandered in the wilderness. It concludes with the following passage:

> And the people said to Joshua, "The Lord our God we will serve, and his voice we will obey." So Joshua made a covenant with the people that day, and made statutes and ordinances for them at Shechem. And Joshua wrote these words in the book of the law of God; and he took a great stone, and set it up there under the oak in the sanctuary of the Lord. And Joshua said to all the people, "Behold, this stone shall be a witness against us; for it has heard all the words of the Lord which he spoke to us; therefore it shall be a witness against you, lest you deal falsely with your God." So Joshua sent the people away, every man to his inheritance. (vv.24-28)

On "that day" Joshua "made statutes and ordinances *for them*," which ended in the form of "the book of the law of God." Although we are not privy to those statutes and ordinances, the unavoidable conclusion is that Joshua re-read to the hearing of the people assembled at Shechem what was earlier read at Mounts Gerizim and Ebal (8:33) as Moses had preordained (Deut 27:4). The relation between the two episodes finds confirmation in the similar wording: "And there, in the presence of the people of Israel, he wrote upon the stones a copy of the law of Moses, which he had written." (Josh 8:32) Moses' instruction is part of "the words of the covenant which the Lord

commanded Moses to make with the people of Israel in the land
of Moab, besides the covenant which he had made with them at
Horeb" (Deut 29:1). Put otherwise, we are dealing with a series
of renewals of the one Mosaic covenant; the necessity for
renewals is due to the emergence of a new generation or, at least,
a new situation. A basic component in the ceremony of renewal
is the remembrance of the crossing of the Red Sea and the trek in
the wilderness (vv.2-7). This is precisely what we also find in
Joshua 24:2-13. However, in this case, the recollection of the
divine past actions includes the entrance into Canaan (vv.11-13)
which, for obvious reasons, was not part of the covenant renewal
ceremony at Moab.

However, this recollection is not simply a mental exercise. Its
function is to make the hearers partakers of the original events,
which is clearly the case in Joshua 24. In the instance of the
additional event, the entrance into Canaan, which only applies
to Joshua's addressees, the recipients of God's deeds are spoken
to in the second person plural:

> Then I brought you to the land of the Amorites, who lived on the
> other side of the Jordan; they fought with you, and I gave them
> into your hand, and you took possession of their land, and I
> destroyed them before you. Then Balak the son of Zippor, king of
> Moab, arose and fought against Israel; and he sent and invited
> Balaam the son of Beor to curse you, but I would not listen to
> Balaam; therefore he blessed you; so I delivered you out of his
> hand. And you went over the Jordan and came to Jericho, and the
> men of Jericho fought against you, and also the Amorites, the
> Perizzites, the Canaanites, the Hittites, the Girgashites, the
> Hivites, and the Jebusites; and I gave them into your hand. And I
> sent the hornet before you, which drove them out before you, the
> two kings of the Amorites; it was not by your sword or by your
> bow. I gave you a land on which you had not labored, and cities

which you had not built, and you dwell therein; you eat the fruit of vineyards and oliveyards which you did not plant. (vv.8-13)

In the rendition of the exodus, there is a back-and-forth between the second person and the third person:

And I sent Moses and Aaron, and I plagued Egypt with what I did in the midst of it; and afterwards I brought *you* out. Then I brought *your fathers* out of Egypt, and *you* came to the sea; and the Egyptians pursued *your fathers* with chariots and horsemen to the Red Sea (Red Sea). And when *they* cried to the Lord, he put darkness between *you* and the Egyptians, and made the sea come upon them and cover them; and *your* eyes saw what I did to Egypt; and *you* lived in the wilderness a long time. (vv.5-7)

Such integration of the hearers into the narrative is a normal phenomenon we experience when we feel engaged in listening to a story or watching a movie; we often end up being "one" with the character of our choice. However, in the scriptural recollection, we are *forced* into that role, as is clear from the last passage (vv.5-7).[1] But the question is, "To what purpose?" Listening intently to the passage, one will notice that the main agent of the deeds is the Lord himself, while the other personalities are mere recipients of the effect of those deeds, with two exceptions: "Your fathers lived of old beyond the Euphrates, Terah, the father of Abraham and of Nahor; and they served other gods ... but Jacob and his children went down to Egypt." (vv.2b, 4b) What is most important in both these cases is that the actions are against God's will: serving other gods and going

---

[1] Another well-known instance is 1 Cor 10:1 where Paul forces the Corinthian Gentiles into being the children of the scriptural "fathers": "I want you to know, brethren, that our fathers were all under the cloud, and all passed through the sea."

down to Egypt.[2] The moral of such a story is that if the hearers are co-recipients of God's gifts *in the story*, they are, by the same token, responsible not to fall prey to the mistakes of the protagonists *in that same story*. This is confirmed by scripture itself. In the first part of Joshua's concluding remarks is the following invitation: "Now therefore fear the Lord, and serve him in sincerity and in faithfulness; *put away the gods which your fathers served beyond the River, and in Egypt*, and serve the Lord. And if you be unwilling to serve the Lord, choose this day whom you will serve, whether *the gods your fathers served in the region beyond the River*, or *the gods of the Amorites in whose land you dwell*." (vv.14-15a) This warning presents two main points:

1. Abraham was not, on the factual level, a monotheist, as much of biblical scholarship still assumes. Moreover, his progeny kept serving "the gods beyond the River" not only in Canaan but also in Egypt. Even more, the following generations kept that tradition up to that moment, since Joshua is asking those gathered at Shechem to "*put away* the gods which your fathers served beyond the River, and in Egypt."

2. The people can still opt for serving similar deities, e.g., the gods of the Amorites surrounding them, rather than putting away those gods.

So Joshua is asking the people to set aside all "harlotry" consisting in following any other gods; after all, it is the Lord God who kept taking care of them in spite of their continual

---

[2] Jacob went down to Egypt seeking bread during a famine in Canaan, instead of waiting for bread from the Lord; see my comments in *C-Gen* 174-5.

unfaithfulness. However, now that they are settled and "at rest" in Canaan, they are facing their last chance: either they accept to live according to the "statutes and ordinances" of that God (v.25) or "the Lord will bring upon you all the evil things, until he have destroyed you from off this good land which the Lord your God has given you, if you transgress the covenant of the Lord your God, which he commanded you, and go and serve other gods and bow down to them. Then the anger of the Lord will be kindled against you, and you shall perish quickly from off the good land which he has given to you" (23:15-16)

Likewise, they are to "choose *this day*," the day in which Joshua and his house have chosen (24:15). That is to say, the choice to serve the Lord is to be made expressly family by family, and the hearers know exactly what that means since they were just reminded (22:20) of the fate of "Achan the son of Zerah, and the silver and the mantle and the bar of gold, and his sons and daughters, and his oxen and asses and sheep, and his tent, and all that he had" (7:24). Now that they have committed themselves (24:16-18), they are again reminded of the threat awaiting them and which they just heard (23:15-16): "You cannot serve the Lord; for he is a holy God; he is a jealous God; he will not forgive your transgressions or your sins. If you forsake the Lord and serve foreign gods, then he will turn and do you harm, and consume you, after having done you good." (24:19-20) As if their repeated acquiescence (v.21) was not enough, Joshua makes them aware that they stand as witnesses against themselves (v.22). Only after acceptance of such they are asked to officially "put away the foreign gods which are among you" (v.23a), which is tantamount to an open confession on their part that they were still holding to "the gods of their fathers." What irony! It is as though the author wanted to make us, the hearers of the text, aware that the original addressees were "caught in the act."

Hearers of the text should then beware when their turn comes, especially that they are privy to the rest of the story of the Prior Prophets!

The Death of Joshua

Only now is Joshua's mission fulfilled (vv.25-28) and he may "go the way of all the earth" (23:14), that is, die (24:29). He is given the special blessing of being buried in his own inheritance (v.30). The following remark is double-edged: "And Israel served the Lord all the days of Joshua, and all the days of the elders who outlived Joshua and had known all the work which the Lord did for Israel." (v.31) On the one hand, it gives the impression that it is complimenting the people for having indeed "served the Lord" and thus for having kept the solemn oath they just took. On the other hand, it is also continuing the honor bestowed upon Joshua in the previous verse by reminding the hearers that he and his elders kept the people on the right track. However, the hearers will soon fully realize the full impact of the latter meaning when less than two chapters later the following passage will resound:

> And the people served the Lord all the days of Joshua, and all the days of the elders who outlived Joshua, who had seen all the great work which the Lord had done for Israel. And Joshua the son of Nun, the servant of the Lord, died at the age of one hundred and ten years. And they buried him within the bounds of his inheritance in Timnathheres, in the hill country of Ephraim, north of the mountain of Gaash. And all that generation also were gathered to their fathers; and there arose another generation after them, who did not know the Lord or the work which he had done for Israel. And the people of Israel did what was evil in the sight of the Lord and served the Baals; and they forsook the Lord, the God of their fathers, who had brought them out of the land of Egypt;

they went after other gods, from among the gods of the peoples who were round about them, and bowed down to them; and they provoked the Lord to anger. (Judg 2:7-12)

A keen ear used to the unexpected scriptural "twists" can detect dark clouds on the horizon in the last two verses of Joshua that mention the interment of Joseph's bones and the death and burial of the high priest Eleazar. Just as Moses the lawgiver is no more and only his teaching remains, so also Joseph, the savior of both Israel and Egypt, is no more; only his bones remain. Although his presence among the people may sound reassuring, still the place of his burial is ominous. "The portion of ground which Jacob bought from the sons of Hamor the father of Shechem for a hundred pieces of money" (24:32; see Gen 33:18-20) is where Joseph's older brothers, Simeon and Levi, "have brought trouble (*'akartem*; from the verb *'akar* used in conjunction with Achan's sin) on me [Jacob] by making me odious to the inhabitants of the land, the Canaanites and the Perizzites; my numbers are few, and if they gather themselves against me and attack me, I shall be destroyed, both I and my household" (34:30) Moreover their hideous crime was that they misused circumcision, the sign of the covenant through which Abraham was made "the father of a multitude of nations" (Gen 17:5). They forced the Shechemites to be circumcised, then killed those "circumcised brethren" and plundered the homes (34:25-29) of the same people who sold Jacob the piece of land that was to become the burial site of Joseph's bones.

As for the death of Eleazar, it announces a full amnesty to all unintentional perpetrators of homicide (Josh 20:6), thus reminding the people that "As I live, says the Lord God, I have no pleasure in the death of the wicked, but that the wicked turn from his way and live; turn back, turn back from your evil ways;

for why will you die, O house of Israel?" (Ezek 33:11; see also 18: 23, 32). Now the people are left on their own to choose their fate.

Further Reading

Commentaries and Studies

Harris J. G., Brown C. A. and Moore M. S. *Joshua, Judges, Ruth*. NIBC OT 5. Peabody, MA: Hendrickson; Carlisle, UK: Paternoster, 2000.

Harstad. A. L. *Joshua*. Concordia Commentary. St Louis: Concordia Publishing House, 2004.

Hawk, L. D. *Joshua*. Collegeville, MN: Liturgical Press, 2000.

Oden, T. C. and Franke, J. R. *Joshua, Judges, Ruth, 1-2 Samuel*. Downers Grove, IL: InterVarsity Press, 2005.

Pressler, C. *Joshua, Judges, and Ruth*. Westminster Bible Companion. Louisville/London: Westminster John Knox, 1996.

Articles

Angel, H. "There Is No Chronological Order in the Torah: An Axiom for Understanding the book of Joshua." *The Jewish Bible Quarterly* 36 (2008) 3-11.

Assis E. "The Position and Function of Jos 22 in the Book of Joshua." *Zeitschrift für die alttestamentliche Wissenschaft* 116 (2004) 528-41.

Batto, B. "Images of God in Joshua and Judges." *The Bible Today* 39 (2001) 217-23.

Beck, J. E. "Why Do Joshua's Readers Keep Crossing the River? The Narrative-Geographical Shaping of Joshua 3-4." *Journal of the Evangelical Theological Society* 48 (2005) 689-99.

Butticaz, S. "Josué et la rhétorique de la violence: le cas de la prise d'Aï en Josué 8/1-29." *Etudes Théologiques et Religieuses* 77 (2002) 421-27.

Earl, D. "Reading the Book of Joshua Theologically: The Problem of Violence." *Scripture Bulletin* 35 (2005) 61-72.

Frolov, S. "Joshua's Double Demise (Josh xxiv 28-32; Judg ii 6-9): Making Sense of a Repetition." *Vetus Testamentum* 58 (2008) 315-23.

Hawk, L. D. "Fixing Boundaries: The Construction of Identity in Joshua." *Ashland Theological Journal* 32 (2000) 21-31.

Hawk, L. D. "Undivided Inheritance and Lot Casting in the Book of Joshua." *Journal of Biblical Literature* 119 (2000) 601-18.

Hawk, L. D. "The God of the Conquest: The Theological Problem of the Book of Joshua." *The Bible Today* 46 (2008) 141-47.

Hens-Piazza, G. "Violence in Joshua and Judges." *The Bible Today* 39 (2001) 196-203.

Hess, R. S. "The Book of Joshua as a Land Grant." *Biblica* 83 (2002) 493-506.

Merling D. "The Book of Joshua, Part I: Its Evaluation by Nonevidence." *Andrews University Seminary Studies* 39 (2001) 61-72.

Merling D. "The Book of Joshua, Part II: Expectations of Archaeology." *Andrews University Seminary Studies* 39 (2001) 209-21.

Merling D. "Rahab: The Woman Who Fulfilled the Word of YHWH." *Andrews University Seminary Studies* 41 (2003) 31-44.

Pienaar D. N. "Some Observations on Conquest Reports in the Book of Joshua." *Journal of Northwest Semitic Languages* 30 (2004) 151-64.

Rösel M. "The Septuagint-Version of the Book of Joshua." *Scandinavian Journal of the Old Testament* 16 (2002) 5-23.

Sherwood, A. "A Leader's Misleading and a Prostitute Profession: A Reexamination of Joshua 2." *Journal for the Study of the Old Testament* 31 (2006) 43-61.

Spina, F. A. "Reversal of Fortune." *Bible Review* 17 (2001) 24-30, 53-54.

Stek, J. H. "Rahab of Canaan and Israel: The Meaning of Joshua 2." *Calvin Theological Journal* 37 (2002) 28-48.

Strange, J. "The Book of Joshua—Origin and Dating." *Journal for the Study of the Old Testament* 28 (2000) 52-55.

CPSIA information can be obtained at www.ICGtesting.com
Printed in the USA
BVOW02s1647160316

440530BV00001B/57/P